The Essential Guide to

GOLF
TECHNIQUES

Everything you need to improve your game

igloobooks

THE ESSENTIAL GUIDE TO
GOLF
TECHNIQUES

EVERYTHING YOU NEED TO IMPROVE YOUR GAME

PHIL BONSALL

FOREWORD BY
JOHN JACOBS

Published in 2015
by Igloo Books Ltd
Cottage Farm
Sywell
NN6 OBJ
www.igloobooks.com

SHE001 0715
2 4 6 8 10 9 7 5 3 1
ISBN: 978-1-78440-201-3

Photographer: Mark Winwood
Model: Christopher Winwood

Photographed at La Toree Golf Resort, part of the Polaris World Nicklaus
Golf Trail, Mucia, Spain

Cover and endpaper images © Thinkstock / Getty Images

Printed and manufactured in China

CONTENTS

FOREWORD

Teaching golf as I have done now for many enjoyable years – too many, some would say – I recognise the importance of individuality. We are all different, and so are our golf swings. But the forces that we need to apply to the golf ball in order to play the game consistently and well are the same and will always remain so. These forces – or fundamentals, laws, and principles – are described clearly in this book, giving the reader a very good understanding of the basics that are required to start and enjoy a lifetime's game. But these pages provide more than just technical information – they cover all aspects of the game, from shot shaping to sand play, from putting to power, and much more.

To learn golf also requires structure. Having a consistent process that, when used, quickly gives answers to problems, can prove invaluable and extremely useful for players of any standard. With his unique use of the GASPS (Grip, Aim and alignment, Stance, Posture and ball position, and Swing) system, the author of this book hands the player the necessary tools to identify and correct faults as they occur.

Along with structured learning come three key elements or questions that I feel make players improve and become successful: firstly, are the players "coach-able", open to advice, and willing to change?; secondly, do they perform well under pressure and enjoy the competitive side of the game?; and, finally, do they practise correctly?

The last point is extremely important. I so often witness, now on a daily basis, players practising their faults rather than practising using the knowledge that they need in order to improve. With the excellent drills that accompany the many sections of this book, practising constructively and correctly will become second nature to the golfer. The drills will assist them in moving the ball consistently and correctly while they are playing and practising, and instill in them the knowledge they need in order to improve. Not only does this book give excellent factual information but, more

importantly, it is written using an organised and structured approach, making it easier for the golfer to learn the game.

This guide is your "written personal coach", available whenever you need it. I just wish I could be that accessible! Many influences have guided me toward coaching, and nothing has done so more aptly than the advice given by top tournament professional Greg Norman. The advice he gave was DIN and DIP: "do it now" and "do it properly". I made the decision to follow this structure in my coaching, and his advice is clearly echoed within these pages. If a player follows the instruction given here, not only will changes take effect quickly, but they will also be sustained, standing the test of time.

We never stop learning and, after reading this book, I have undertaken many of the drills to assist my own coaching and game. They have proved both valuable and fun, which I'm sure was the original intention – thank you.

John Jacobs

John Jacobs works as a coach with many top amateur players plus professionals. He has also been chosen as one of 25 top golfers to write regularly for Golf Monthly.

Each golfer will have their own unique style, but the fundamentals of the game remain the same and every golfer must learn them.

HOW TO USE THIS BOOK

Golf is a sport that anybody can enjoy learning to play, whatever their age or sporting ability. However, no matter what ability a player has, they will sometimes have difficulty remembering exactly what they are meant to be doing, especially once the lesson has ended and they are practising by themselves. In order to combat this problem, this book will introduce you to the GASPS system.

You can remember this system by thinking that everyone will "gasp" with amazement at your newfound ability and improved technique! This is a tried-and-tested method that pros have been using for many years with great success.

Starting with the first chapter, which is dedicated to the set up, this system is the basis for the entire book. You will be taught the Grip, how to Aim, the correct Stance, good Posture and how to Swing for every shot.

For each of the different shots in the book, the techniques are described in the order listed above. This will aid you in your learning, and also make it easy to remember when you don't have the book with you.

Every time you hit a shot, you should think "GASPS" and go through the routine in your mind to ensure that you are doing everything in the right order.

If you follow the advice in this book closely, and give yourself the chance to practise and learn at each stage, there will be no doubt that your game will improve.

The first half of the book deals with learning the correct technique for all the shots you will need to play the game, and the second half of the book deals with actually playing the game, together with common faults and fixes that can creep into your technique.

As valuable as this book will hopefully be to your game, regular lessons from a Professional Golfers' Association (PGA) qualified professional are advised, to supplement the advice given. PGA professionals are trained to help you with your game, and a course of lessons is a great investment. Tiger Woods still has regular lessons, as do most PGA Tour professionals. If it is good enough for them, it should be good enough for you.

Working together with this book, and with a PGA professional, you will definitely see improvement.

We can't all swing like a professional, but by following the GASPS system and putting in the practice, you will lower your handicap – guaranteed!

GASPS STANDS FOR

GRIP

How to hold the club is the most important lesson in the entire book. Without the correct grip it is impossible to make a good swing. Get it right now, and it will serve you well for your entire golfing life.

AIM AND ALIGNMENT

Aim and alignment are factors you can control before you swing, and they deserve extra attention. Get a good grip to a square clubface, aim the clubface, and align your body, in that order.

STANCE

Having the correct golf stance gives you stable footing throughout your swing and puts you in better control of the ball. The position of your feet and your posture affects the angle of your swing, which strongly determines the direction of your ball.

POSTURE AND BALL POSITION

Posture, stance, and ball position are very closely related. Positioning the golf ball correctly in your stance is fundamental to every great shot. A beginner will start by learning where the ball is in relation to his or her feet.

SWING

Without a doubt the most important aspect of golf is the swing. The proper golf swing can be divided into three segments: the backswing; the downswing; and the impact and follow through.

THE BASICS

CLOTHING

Modern golf clothing utilises the latest synthetic fabrics and, like golf shoes, comes in a bewildering array of styles and colours – there should be something for just about everyone. Remember, the most important thing is comfort and practicality. Your clothes should not restrict your swing but should provide sufficient protection against the elements.

SHOES

Golf shoes in particular have improved immensely in recent years. New waterproofing materials and different types of spikes have made them much more comfortable and you can get just about any colour. When buying shoes, remember that comfort is paramount. Playing 18 holes on a standard golf course is the equivalent of walking approximately 5–6 miles (7–8km), so ensure you get a pair of shoes that are a good fit and offer good support.

If you play golf all year round and the area where you live undergoes seasonal change, you may want to consider buying a lighter-weight shoe for the summer and a heavier, more waterproof shoe for the winter.

You should also be aware of the type of spikes the shoes can be fitted with. Many courses, particularly in warm, dry countries, only allow soft spikes, while in more temperate countries, particularly in winter, metal spikes may be most effective at stopping you from slipping as you swing.

CLOTHING

If you live in an area that receives a lot of rainfall – and many golfers around the world do – you will need a good set of waterproofs. Staying dry and comfortable will not only help you to enjoy yourself more, but will also ensure you play at your best. When buying waterproofs, make sure that they are lightweight and, like the rest of your clothes, do not restrict your swing. If in doubt, try them on and then ask if you can go outside and make a few swings.

GOLF GLOVES

A golf glove, while not essential, will help you to grip the club and prevent it turning in your hands. Most players only wear one glove, on the top or leading hand. Gloves are made of a variety of materials, leather and/or synthetic and should be a close fit on the hand while still allowing the fingers to be freely flexible.

Comfortable golf shoes are essential.

Choose clothing that doesn't restrict you as you swing the golf club.

There are golf clothes to suit just about every taste.

GOLF CLUBS AND BALLS

As any enthusiastic golfer will tell you, buying golf clubs is great fun. You can get a real buzz from buying a new driver, putter or iron – hoping, of course, that your new purchase will help to bring down your score! In years gone by, a set of clubs was fairly standard – most of them comprised three woods (1, 3 and 5), nine irons (3–9, wedge and sand wedge) and a putter. Recently, however, there have been plenty of innovations in club design and players now have a variety of different types of club to choose from. New materials and manufacturing processes have also meant that there now really is a ball to suit all players.

Perhaps the greatest innovation in club technology are the hybrid clubs (also known as utility or rescue clubs). A cross between a wood and an iron, these clubs have become widely used by players of all abilities. "Long" irons (3- and 4-irons) have traditionally been the hardest to use, and hybrids are an alternative. They offer a higher flight and, for most people, are much easier to hit. Even the majority of PGA Tour Professionals have switched from long irons to hybrids.

Other recent changes in clubs have seen the introduction of more "lofted" woods such as 7- or 9-woods ("loft" is the measurement of the angle of the clubhead). These are very popular with women players, but should not be discounted by male players. They are designed to go high and then stop fairly quickly when they land, thus offering greater control, while delivering good distance at the same time. A 7-wood offers similar distance to a 3- or 4-iron.

CLUBHEAD SIZE

An important consideration to make when buying irons is the clubhead size. Generally, irons come in three sizes – oversize, midsize and blade or traditional. For those new to the game, oversize clubs are more forgiving and offer a larger "sweet" spot. Midsize clubs are slightly harder to hit, but offer more control over the ball, while traditional "blades" are for lower handicap players who can hit the ball consistently well and want maximum control and feel.

WEDGES

Wedges have changed and increased in number. There used to be two wedges available – the pitching wedge (with approximately 50 degrees of loft) and the sand wedge (with approximately 55 degrees of loft). In a modern set of clubs, the lofts have changed slightly so that the pitching wedge has about 48 degrees of loft. Because of

this there are now many more wedges available. There is a "gap wedge" that is designed to fit between the pitching wedge and sand wedge – so called because it filled the "gap" created when the pitching wedge loft was lowered.

Possibly the biggest advancement in short game technology is the lob wedge. The lob wedge has 60 degrees of loft, so enabling you to "throw" the ball very high and get it to stop very quickly.

As you can see, there are many options when it comes to making up the correct set of clubs to suit your game. Experiment with the various options to see which works best for you and always take advice from a PGA Professional – who is trained to be able to give you the best advice to help your game – before making an expensive purchase.

GOLF BALLS

Possibly the biggest advancement in the game over recent years is in the golf ball. Seek advice from your local professional as to which type of ball would suit your game best. Whatever ball you decide to use, it will really help you to try and use the same sort every time you play. Different balls are designed to play differently and if you keep changing you will find it difficult to become consistent. Find a ball that you like within your price range, and then stick with it.

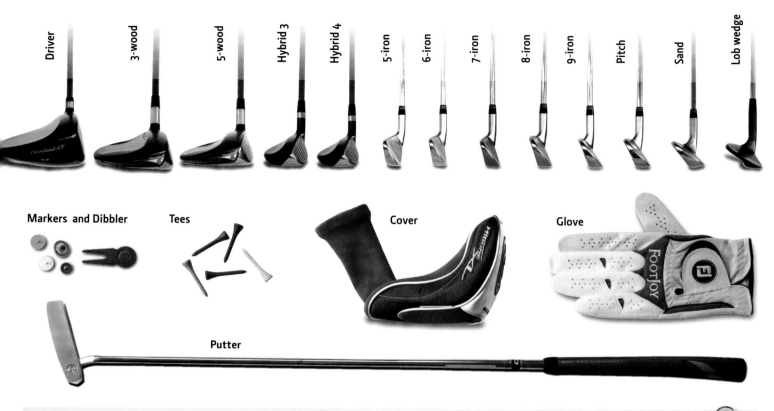

Driver · 3-wood · 5-wood · Hybrid 3 · Hybrid 4 · 5-iron · 6-iron · 7-iron · 8-iron · 9-iron · Pitch · Sand · Lob wedge

Markers and Dibbler

Tees

Cover

Glove

Putter

SUGGESTED SET OF CLUBS

A suggested set of clubs for the average male golfer, taking advantages of all modern technology and ideas, may include the items listed below. A female golfer might choose a 7-wood in place of a 3-hybrid.

- Driver – approximately 10 degrees of loft. For shots off the tee.

- 3-wood – approximately 15 degrees of loft. Tee and long fairway shots.

- 5-wood – approximately 19 degrees of loft. Long fairway shots.

- 3-hybrid – 21 degrees of loft. Long fairway and approach shots.

- 4-hybrid – 24 degrees of loft. Long to mid-approach shots.

- 5-iron – 28 degrees of loft. Mid-approach shots.

- 6-iron – 32 degrees of loft. Mid-approach shots.

- 7-iron – 36 degrees of loft. Mid-approach shots.

- 8-iron – 40 degrees of loft. Mid-short approach shots.

- 9-iron – 44 degrees of loft. Short approach shots.

- Pitching wedge – 48 degrees of loft. Short approach shots.

- Sand wedge – 54 degrees of loft. For playing out of sandtraps.

- Lob wedge – 60 degrees of loft. Very short approach shots.

- Putter – no loft. For putting the ball on the green into the hole.

The above is for guideline purposes only. If you're just starting out, you may find buying a half set (for example, 3-wood, 3-hybrid, 5-iron, 7-iron, 9-iron, sand wedge and putter) is all you need. You can always add to your set as and when you think you need to.

THE COURSE

Golf courses are usually areas of well-manicured grasses in beautiful surroundings, where you can often find many different types of wildlife living in harmony with the golfers. Most courses consist of 18 holes – a standard round of golf – although some have nine holes, which can be played twice to make up a round. Other courses have 27 or 36 holes, allowing a combination of two nine-hole sections to make up a round; this provides variety and helps with the maintenance of the golf course.

To become a good player it is essential that you try many varied types and styles of course – this will help you develop a good all-round game. There are various types of courses.

LINKS COURSES
Links land is land that has been reclaimed from the sea, so true links courses are without exception found on the coast. The early golf courses in Scotland, the oldest in the world, were all links courses and the British Open is still always played over a traditional links course. The characteristics of a links course are that they are usually predominantly flat with small humps and hollows. The turf is usually very fine

and the ground quite firm. The firmness of the ground dictates that you need to run and bounce your ball to its target – on such ground it is difficult to get backspin and make the ball stop. Deep pot bunkers are the biggest hazard of a links course and there is usually a lot of wind to contend with.

PARKLAND COURSES
These courses usually are lined with trees and are a little bit softer under foot than a links course. The key to playing them well is usually accuracy rather than distance, to avoid the trees. Positioning your ball well from the tee leads to an easy approach to the green.

HEATHLAND COURSES
Some of the finest heathland courses are found in southern England and Australia. They can be beautiful places to play golf. The fairways are usually lined with heather and bracken and there are often many pine trees. Similar to links courses in that the ground is often firm, these courses require a good strategy to avoid the heather.

STADIUM COURSES
These courses are increasingly popular, particularly in the United States. Modern earthmoving equipment allows generally flat pieces of land to be manipulated to add contours and hills. There are usually several water hazards on a stadium course and the key to playing them well is to avoid the water! They are often longer courses than the more traditional designs and feature elements such as buggy paths to cope with the demands of the modern golfer.

Tiger Woods on the 15th at St Andrews, the archetypal links course.

The "cuts" of a golf hole – rough, fairway, fringe and green – are visible here.

Despite the many different types of golf course, the aim remains the same. Get the ball in the hole in the fewest possible shots. Whatever the type of course, they all have the following features in common:

TEES
The closely mown area where you start each hole. The teeing ground is the only place on the course where you are allowed to use a tee peg to give your ball the perfect lie. All courses have different tees for men and women, to try and make the game as fair as possible.

FAIRWAYS
The area we are all trying to hit from the tee! The fairway is the short grass between the tee and the green.

SEMIROUGH
Most courses have a strip of semirough on the edge of the fairways. The grass is still relatively short, so if you just miss the fairway you are not punished too severely.

ROUGH
If you miss the fairway and the semirough you will find yourself in the rough. This is longer grass, and is meant to punish you for hitting a wayward shot, by making your next shot more difficult.

APRON OR FRINGE
This is short grass around the edge of the green. If you land on this you have to make a decision on whether to chip or putt. More often than not a putt will be the safest option.

GREENS
The most important part of the course and with the shortest grass. Greens are usually very smooth – to putt well on them, you need to read the subtle undulations.

BUNKERS
Holes in the ground with sand in the bottom. A bunker is a hazard and is designed to make controlling the ball difficult.

OUT OF BOUNDS
This is usually the perimeter of the golf course, but sometimes, for safety reasons, you may find "internal out of bounds", which stops players hitting to the wrong fairway where other golfers may be already playing. Out of bounds is marked by a series of white posts.

WATER HAZARDS
There are two types of water hazard: one is simply called a "water hazard" and is marked by yellow stakes around the edge of it; the other is called a "lateral water hazard" and is defined by red stakes.

THE SET UP

THE SET UP

The overall position you assume before striking the ball will dictate how well you play the shot. Golfers call this position the set up. Getting the set up right is the most important of all the techniques and needs to be learned first. A correct set up is vital for success. If you get the opportunity to watch really good players, you will see various different swings and techniques, but they will all have certain key positions in common. The first of these is the set up.

Do not be under any illusion – golf is a difficult game. This is primarily because the ball is stationary and you have to add power, distance and height from a static position. However, one thing that a still ball allows is for you to be in the right position every time you hit it. In the majority of ball games, the ball is moving when it comes to you, and you have to react to make contact. This can mean poor balance, poor posture and so on. In golf, however, you have the time to make sure you are always set up correctly. It is vital that you make good use of that time.

As you go read through all the techniques, you will notice what an important role the set up plays at every stage. The various types of shot you'll learn all start with the correct position, and by slightly changing this you will dramatically change your results. Let the set up dictate how you swing and you will become a good player. Set up incorrectly and you will forever be searching for a swing to compensate. If you have a poor starting position, you will never master the consistency required to become a good player.

Over the next few pages you will learn the GASPS system: how to Grip the club, how to Aim the club and align your body, the correct Stance and good Posture, and where to position the ball in your stance before you Swing.

GRIP

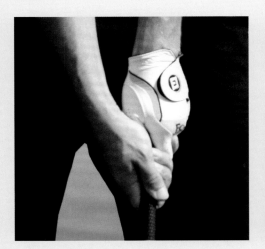

As you take hold on the club make sure you do not grip too tight.

AIM

Once you have picked a suitable target, slowly look from your target to the golf ball and find a spot on the same line near the golf ball.

STANCE

The feet should be roughly shoulder width apart. The target-side foot should be flared toward the target at 20 degrees to allow the body to rotate toward the target.

Learn these positions carefully. If you're new to the game, they will certainly feel strange to begin with, but once you have adopted them for a couple of weeks, they will start to feel natural. Don't let yourself slip into poor habits at this point. Take the time to learn them properly and you will be in great shape to master other techniques.

Refer back to this chapter if things start going consistently wrong. Most swing faults stem back to set up problems that can arise over time without you even realising it. If you're having problems, check all the positions outlined over the next few pages. Correct any faults that may have crept in, and your game will be back on track in no time.

Keep your eye on the ball throughout the duration of the swing.

POSTURE

Weight is evenly distributed on the balls of the feet, not too much toward the toes or the heels. Bend from the hips, allowing the spine to remain relatively straight. Slightly flex your knees.

SWING

Once you have set up and feel confident in your stance, foot and ball position, posture and arm position, you are ready to swing. Always take a few practice swings to make sure everything feels smooth.

THE GRIP

How you hold the club is one of the most fundamental elements of golf to get right. Without the correct grip, it is impossible to make a good swing. Get it right in the first place and it will serve you well for your entire golfing life. A good grip allows the hands to work together in the swing, ensuring you hit the ball accurately and generate power. Wrist action is a power source and gripping the club too much in the palm of your hand reduces wrist action.

First, before you grip the club it is vital that you ensure the face of the club is pointing directly at the target. When you have done this, you will now be looking down at the middle of the grip.

Start with the top hand first; this is the left hand for right-handed players and the right hand for left-handed players. Place it toward the top of the grip, leaving approximately ½in (just over 1cm) of the club sticking out at the top. The thumb of the top hand should be placed just to the right of centre on the grip, and there should be no gap left between the thumb and main part of the hand. If the top hand is in the correct position, you should be able to see the knuckles on the first two or three fingers.

There are three different ways of putting the bottom hand on the grip. Try experimenting with all three grips. See which feels best to you and, more importantly, see which one gives you the best results when you start to hit the ball. See below for the different types of grip.

THE LEFT HAND GRIP

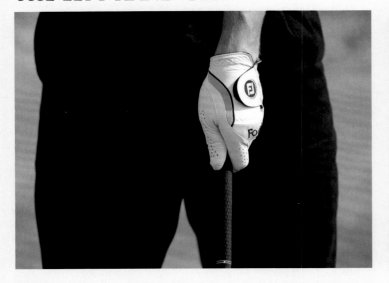

Whichever grip you feel most comfortable with, always place the top hand on the grip first and check that you can see the knuckles of the first two or three fingers before bringing the lower hand down.

THE BASEBALL GRIP

Place the bottom hand on the grip directly under the top hand. The little finger of your bottom hand should literally be touching the forefinger of your top hand. The grip should be in the fingers of the bottom hand, and the bottom thumb should be placed just to the left of centre. This grip is suggested for juniors, women, or men with small hands.

GRIP TIPS

- Always keep the clubface square when you take your grip.

- Show two to three knuckles on your top hand.

- Do not grip too tightly.

A correct golf grip is essential in order to strike the ball well.

THE OVERLAPPING OR VARDON

This is the most popular grip among the tour pros. Take the grip as for the Baseball Grip, then lift up the little finger of the bottom hand from the grip. Close up the space that is now left between the hands, and let the little finger rest in the join between the first two fingers of the top hand.

THE INTERLOCKING GRIP

Made popular by Jack Nicklaus, and more recently by Tiger Woods, this grip is very similar to the Vardon Grip, but instead of resting the little finger of the bottom hand on top of the top hand, you should actually interlock it with the forefinger of the top hand.

ALIGNMENT AND AIM

It may sound obvious, but aiming both the club and your body accurately at the target is vital for successful golf shots. There is no point having a great grip and swing if you haven't lined up properly. It is amazing how many times you will see good golfers really confused and at a loss as to why every shot they are hitting is either going to the right or left. So often it is because they are aiming incorrectly and don't even realise it! So let's take a look at how you can ensure you're aiming exactly at where you want to hit the ball.

To enable you to achieve a repetitive and consistent aim and alignment position, it is vital for you to observe the following sequence:

❶ Aim the club at the target. To enable you to do this accurately, you should visualise a line drawn from just behind the ball, running all the way through to the target. This is called the ball-to-target line.

❷ Place the head of the club on the back of the line, as close as possible to the ball without touching it. The bottom line of the clubhead should be pointing directly at the target, in other words, at a 90-degree angle to the ball-to-target line.

❸ Once the clubhead is in place, visualise another line on the ground. This one will run parallel to the ball-to-target

line at a distance apart similar to that of railroad tracks. Place your feet on this line so that your feet are parallel to the ball-to-target line. In reality, your feet are now aimed just to the left (or right if you're left-handed) of where you want to hit the ball. This is perfect. Do not make the common mistake of thinking that your feet should point directly at the target. If they do, then your club will actually be aimed to the right (or left for left-handers).

❹ Once your feet are in place, try and feel that your knees, hips, and shoulders are all aligned. It is quite common

Visualise the ball-to-target line (see step 1).

Place the clubhead at 90 degrees to the ball-to-target line (see step 2).

for people to have their feet aimed in the right place, and yet their shoulders point completely in a different direction. Ask a friend to stand behind you and check that your feet, knees, hips, and shoulders are all parallel to the ball-to-target line. This is essential for you to start swinging on the correct line.

When you first attempt this, or when you are practising and checking your alignment, it is a good idea to put a club on the ground between your feet and the ball. Make sure the club is parallel to your target and it will really help you to line up correctly.

Keep checking the position of the target as you go about setting your body position for the shot.

Ask a friend to check your body is aligned (see step 4).

Placing a club on the ground will help with alignment (see step 4).

STANCE AND BALL POSITION

Now that you have mastered the first two techniques, you should find you have a good grip and your hands work well together. You should be aiming the clubface directly at the target and aligning your feet and body just to the left (or to the right for left-handers) of the target. The next step is to make sure that you have a good stance, and that the ball is in the correct position in relation to your body. This will allow you to make good clean contact with the ball.

The width of the stance varies slightly, depending on what club you are using. If you are using a 5-, 6- or 7-iron you should stand with your feet shoulder width apart. (Your stance will be wider with a longer club to help you maintain your balance, and slightly narrower with the shorter clubs.)
❶ Start with your feet square to your target line with your toes on the line parallel to the ball-to-target line, as discussed on pages 24–25.
❷ Now slightly turn your front (left) foot out. This will help you to turn your body to the left (or to the right for left-handers) when you start to swing at the ball.

❸ The ball should be positioned just forward of centre in your stance, slightly closer to your front foot than your back foot. This, again, varies depending on the club. As you hit longer clubs, the ball position moves slightly further forward until you reach the driver (the longest of all the clubs), when the ball should be positioned opposite the front heel. As you

Start off with your feet square to the target line ...

... and your toes parallel with the ball-to-target line (see step 1).

hit shots with shorter clubs, the ball moves progressively further back until you reach the wedge (the shortest iron), when the ball will align in the middle of your feet.

❹ The position of your arms is very important. Your front arm should be comfortably straight (not rigid!) and your rear arm should be bent slightly at the elbow. Your rear arm should also rest slightly closer to your body than your front arm. The golf club should form a natural extension of your front arm, and it is very important that with every shot you feel that the back of the front hand is opposite the inside of the front thigh. This will ensure your hands are slightly ahead of the ball, which is vital for a good clean strike.

STANCE TIPS

- Set your feet shoulder width apart for a middle iron. Your stance should be slightly wider for longer clubs, and narrower for shorter clubs.

- Turn your front foot out slightly.

- The ball position should be just forward of centre.

Keep your front arm straight and bend the rear arm slightly at the elbow (see step 4).

With a longer club, your feet should be slightly further apart and the ball positioned further forward (see step 3).

With a shorter club, your feet should be slightly closer together and the ball should be in line with the middle of your feet (see step 3).

POSTURE

Watch any great golf player and you can't help but notice how the golf swing is a supremely elegant yet powerfully athletic motion. To enable you to swing in a similarly athletic fashion, with good rhythm, even tempo and fine balance, it is essential that you start from a position with good posture. This will allow you to make the correct movements freely throughout your swing.

Without good posture, good balance is impossible. Without good balance, a good swing is impossible and, nine times out of ten, a bad swing will result in a bad shot.

When considering posture, let's think about other sports for a moment. Try and visualise a tennis player waiting to receive a serve, or a wrestler about to engage an opponent. They are both standing in an athletic position, ready to move in just about any direction with ease. These are good images to use for golf. It is vital that you have that same poised yet athletic starting position that will allow you to move in both directions easily.

To obtain the correct posture, you should practise the routine shown in the steps opposite. Go through the routine without a ball in front of you. When you have mastered it, you should be able to feel the posture that you should adopt whenever you swing a golf club.

Once you have completed the process shown here, it is a good idea to check your posture in front of a full-length mirror. Check to see that your knees are slightly flexed, your back is angled forward, and that your arms hang freely down. Your hands should be roughly in a position directly below your chin. Do you look athletic and poised? If so, great. If not, repeat the process until you do.

Take hold of the club with your preferred grip (see step 1).

Hold the club out parallel to the ground (see step 2).

❶ Pick up the club, and take your grip as explained on pages 22–23.

❷ Stand up tall with your feet shoulder width apart. Distribute your weight evenly between each foot. Extend your arms comfortably in front of you, holding the club so that the shaft is parallel to the ground at waist height.

❸ Bend forward from the hips, keeping the spine straight, until the clubhead is just short of the ground. At this point, your body weight should automatically move to the balls of your feet.

❹ The backs of your knees will have tightened. Gently flex or soften the knees to remove this tension. Raise your chin up off your chest so that your head is held up slightly.

POSTURE TIPS

• Your posture should be poised and athletic.

• Ensure your knees are soft and not bent rigid.

• Try to relax while holding the posture.

Hold your head up slightly by raising your chin (see step 4)

Bend at the hips, keeping the spine straight (see step 3).

Gently flex your knees, keeping them "soft" (see step 4).

PRE-SHOT ROUTINE

A good pre-shot routine is something that all good players have. You should go through the routine just before you hit every shot. The idea of the pre-shot routine is that it gives you an opportunity to check that you're aiming in the right direction and that your overall body position – including hands, feet, head, shoulders, and so on – is correct before you swing. Each player's routine is slightly different and unique to them, but it is definitely something that all the best players do, and therefore something that you should try to build into your own game.

A pre-shot routine helps to ensure you're in the correct position before you hit each shot and have the correct positive mental image of the shot you are about to play.

Try and watch the best players in the world either live or on television. Pick one player and watch them do the same thing every time they play a shot.

The pre-shot routine in the steps shown opposite is a good starting point, as it addresses all the elements you need to be aware of before you swing. The following routine covers all of the basic points, but don't feel compelled to follow it exactly – add or take away any bits that you want in order to create a routine with which you are comfortable.

Visualise hitting a good shot flying straight to target (see step 1).

Aim the clubface exactly at the intermediate target (see step 5).

❶ Select the club for the shot then walk 2–3yds (about 2–3m) behind the ball so that you are directly in line with the ball and the target. From this position, try and get a picture in your mind of the shot that you want to hit. Visualise a good shot flying straight to your target.

❷ Imagine a line on the ground between the ball and the target (the ball-to-target line).

❸ Pick a spot on this line a couple of yards in front of the ball. It could be a divot, or a little flower, or just an imperfection in the turf. This spot is going to be your "intermediate target".

❹ Go back round to the side of the ball and have a practice swing with the visual image of the good shot fresh in your mind.

❺ Make sure your grip is correct, and then aim the clubface exactly at the intermediate target that you picked out when standing behind the ball. It is much easier to aim at something within a couple of yards of you than your actual target, which could be 200yds (180m) away.

❻ Align your body so that your feet, knees, hips, and shoulders are all parallel to the ball-to-target line and clubface. It is much easier to align your body once you have the clubface in position.

❼ Make sure that you have the ball in the right position, and that your posture and stance are correct.

❽ You should now be in a good position. The last thing you should do before you swing is to look at the intermediate target again to check that you are still aiming correctly, and then look at the actual target. Really focus on where you want the ball to go.

❾ Finally, look back down at the ball, relax as much as possible and make your swing.

PRE-SHOT TIPS

- Ensure you go through your pre-shot routine each time you play a game of golf.

- Practise the routine, changing it slightly to suit you. It should only take about 20 seconds or so to do.

With the clubface correctly positioned and your body aligned, you should now be able to set up your posture and stance (see step 7).

GRIP DRILL

If you have followed and practised the previous techniques, you should now have a good set up position. However, if you're like most people, this position probably feels a little unnatural and awkward. In order to combat this and make the set up feel as natural as possible, and also to make it easier for you to remember and feel the correct positions, there are a few practice exercises that should help (we call these exercises "start-up drills"), beginning with the grip.

When you are learning golf, getting the feeling for the correct grip is vital. Normally, it feels uncomfortable to begin with, but practising this drill will help.

❶ Every time you have a spare ten minutes, just pick up the club, take the correct grip, and get used to having the club in your hands. Put it down, and repeat the process. The more often you do this, the more likely you are to be able to repeat the grip correctly when you play or practise. Relax your hands and arms, and gently waggle the club in front of you. Do not grip too hard – it should feel relaxed and easy.

❷ Take your grip as normal. Bring the club up so that it is waist high, parallel to the ground pointing directly in front of you. If your grip is correct, the toe of the club should point directly to the sky. This is a good way of checking that you are gripping correctly.

❸ If the toe points forward it may mean you have a strong grip. In other words, your hands are too far round to the right (or left for left-handers). This can lead to pulled shots.

❹ If the toe points backward you may have a weak grip, with hands too far round to the left (or right for left-handers), resulting in sliced shots.

THE GRIP

The toe of the club points up with a correct grip (see step 2).

The toe points forward with a strong grip (see step 3).

The toe points backward with a weak grip (see step 4).

POSTURE DRILL

Practise this drill with a friend. It will make you aware of the correct posture to use.

❶ Take your set up position as normal. If your posture is correct, you should have a good feeling of balance and feel athletically poised.

❷ Ask your friend to gently push you from the front of your shoulders. If your balance is good, you should just rock back and forward and return to your set up position. If your posture is wrong, you'll fall backward.

❸ Ask your friend to push you gently from behind. Again, you should just rock forward then back and return to your original starting position. If your balance is incorrect, you will topple forward or back when you are pushed.

If you take the time to practise the set up drills, you will be ready to move on to the next stage, and start to swing the club. If you are more experienced, the exercises will be just as useful to help remind you of the importance of the set up.

In time, good posture will feel natural and come as second nature.

POSTURE

Once you feel comfortable with your posture, ask a friend to push you gently on the front of the shoulders (see step 2).

If you have the correct posture, you should gently rock back and then forward again to your set up position (see step 2).

AIM, ALIGNMENT, AND BALL POSITION DRILL

Every time you go to practise, try placing some clubs on the ground, as this will help enormously with your aim and alignment.

❶ First, set up a ball on the ground, and then place a club approximately 3ft (90cm) in front of it, with the shaft of the club pointing directly at your target.
❷ Place another club on the ground approximately 1½ft (45cm) behind the ball. The shaft of this club should also point directly at your target. These two clubs represent the ball-to-target line.
❸ Now place a third club on the ground, approximately 1½ft (45cm) to the left of the ball. This club should be parallel to the other clubs, and point just to the left of the target. As you set up, you should make sure your feet are

parallel to the third club; doing so will ensure that you are aligned and aimed correctly. This is a great drill – many of the best players in the world use very similar methods to practise aiming correctly.
❹ Place a fourth club on the ground to check your ball position. This one should be placed across the club nearest to your feet so that they form a cross with a 90-degree join. This club should be placed level with the ball so that it points straight at it.

Place a third club on the ground parallel to the first two (see step 3).

Align your feet with the third club (see step 3).

❺ When you take your stance you should make sure that this fourth club is positioned just left of centre between your feet. By doing this, you are ensuring a good ball position every time. If you practise this drill enough, you will eventually find that you automatically place the ball in the correct position when you go to play a shot.

Study the photos of our golfer (above and left) in his set up position, both from the back and the side. Stand in front of a mirror and try and copy the positions as closely as possible.

Place a fourth club over the third to form a cross (see step 4).

THE SWING

THE SWING

It's vital before you progress to the next stage that you're entirely comfortable with the set up position.
If not, practise it a little more before continuing. If you're happy with the set up, the next element of the golf
shot to learn is the swing. Everyone appears to have an opinion as to how you should swing a golf club – there
have been more books written on the golf swing than on any other topic in sport. Each one claims to have
discovered "the magic move" that will make you play like Jack Nicklaus or Tiger Woods.

Unfortunately there is no "magic move", but the golf swing
need not be as complicated as most people think. Over
the next few pages we'll introduce you to a series of
simple moves – simple only if you have the correct set up
position! – that will allow you to get the feel of the swing.
As you start out, the movements may feel a bit forced or
wooden, but once you get used to them you will have a
swing for life.

Imagine throwing a ball as far you can – better still, next
time you're on the practice ground, actually throw a golf
ball. What did you think about as you were throwing?
If you're being honest, the answer is likely nothing. You
probably just focused on where you wanted the ball to go
and then threw it. Throwing a ball requires a sequence of
athletic moves, but it is such a natural thing to do, and
something that you probably did repeatedly as a child, that
you now just do it automatically. This is the feeling we want
to achieve with the golf swing.

You need to learn the few key positions we're going
to show you over the next few pages, and practise them
until they become as natural as throwing a ball. If you can
achieve that same natural feeling when you go out to play
you can just focus on the target and make your swing. It
won't be perfect every time, just like when you throw the
ball sometimes it will not go exactly where you want, but
it will give you a consistent and free swing.

At the end of this chapter there are a series of exercises
and drills that will help you gain a better understanding of
the swing and how it should feel. Take the time to practise
these and you will be a long way toward becoming the
golfer you want to be.

A golf swing should feel as natural as throwing a stone into the ocean – practise it enough and you shouldn't have to think about it.

The last stage of a good golf swing is a well-balanced, final follow through position.

SWING TIPS

- Try to rid your body of any tension when swinging the golf club.

- Swing within yourself with good rhythm and tempo.

- Finish in balance with your weight on your front foot.

THE FIRST MOVE

Now that you've mastered and feel relaxed in the correct set up position, it's important for you to stay relaxed before and as you start to swing the club. Do not allow your body to "freeze" over the ball, as this will create tension and more than likely result in a poor swing and a less-than-satisfactory end result. Good players always make a few small movements prior to starting their swing, which help to relieve tension and ensure the swing starts in a relaxed yet controlled manner.

When you are relaxed and ready to swing, the first movement of the swing is called the "takeaway". It is vital that you move the club, your hands, your arms, and your body all at the same time.

❶ The feeling is one of "sweeping" the club away from the ball. A good way to achieve this is to feel that you're going to gently turn your front shoulder toward your chin as you swing your hands and arms away from the ball.

❷ If you do this correctly you will have the feeling that you are turning your body to the right (or left if you're left-handed). Your body weight should have automatically started to move over to your back foot, your head should have stayed perfectly still and central, and the arms will be comfortably straight.

"Sweep" the club back and away ensuring the club and your hands, arms, and body all move at the same time (see step 1).

By the time you get to the "halfway back" position you should feel your body weight start to move over to your back foot (see step 2).

TAKEAWAY CHECKLIST

To check you are making the initial takeaway movement correctly, you should stop when the club reaches a point where the shaft is parallel to the ground. The points for you to check are as follows:

• The club shaft should lie parallel to an imaginary line drawn along your toes. If the club is behind this line and the clubhead is behind your body, then you have moved the club too quickly to the inside, or around your body. If the club is in front of the line then the club has moved too far to the outside, or away from the body.

• The toe of the club should almost point to the sky. A common mistake is to have the clubface looking down at the ground at this point, which will cause the ball to go left (or right for left-handers) in a full swing.

• Your front knee should have turned in, and now be pointing toward the ball. If done correctly, your weight will have shifted to the back foot, which is perfect. You will now have arrived at the ideal halfway back position.

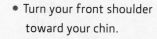

TAKEAWAY TIPS

• Turn your front shoulder toward your chin.

• Feel that everything stays together as you swing away from the ball.

• Ensure that your body weight has shifted toward the back foot.

• Your head should stay fairly still and central.

• Your front arm and the club should have retained a fairly straight line.

The club should naturally start to travel inside the ball-to-target line.

Make sure that the toe of the clubhead is pointing almost directly upward toward the sky.

TOP OF THE BACKSWING

The first stage of the swing, the takeaway, is described on pages 40–41, and ends in a position known as halfway back. The weight has shifted toward the back foot, the arms are comfortably straight, and the shoulders have started to turn to the right (or to the left for left-handers). The swing now continues until you reach the top of the backswing. This is a key position, as it sets the tone for the downswing and impact with the ball. Get it wrong and it can have disastrous consequences on your shots.

As you continue with the backswing, keep turning your shoulders (see step 1).

To get from the halfway back position to the top of the backswing, you need to follow five essential steps to ensure you have adopted the correct position as the club completes the backswing.

❶ Continue turning your shoulders as you swing your hands and arms up and away from your body. The front arm should stay comfortably straight, and the back arm will have folded into a 90-degree angle.

❷ Your body weight should now be heavily on your back foot, with approximately 90% of your weight on your back foot at the top of the backswing. Your front knee will have continued to move back and should now be pointing just behind the ball.

❸ The shaft of the club should be approximately parallel to the ground, and your thumbs should be underneath the grip supporting the club. The back of your front wrist should be flat to your arm.

❹ The angle of your spine should remain constant throughout the backswing, so try and avoid standing up taller as you swing back – this is a very common fault. Visualise and feel a turning sensation. In simple terms, a good backswing just requires you to turn your shoulders 90 degrees to the right as you swing your hands up and away to a position over your back shoulder.

❺ Begin by enacting this move slowly, and repeat it time after time to help reinforce the feeling in your muscles.

TOP OF THE BACKSWING TIPS

- Try to keep your front arm comfortably straight as you take it back.

- Don't stand up taller as you make your backswing.

- Feel your shoulders turning as the club swings back.

The backswing complete, 90% of your weight is on the back foot (see step 2).

The clubshaft should be almost parallel to the ground (see step 3).

THE TRANSITION

The change of direction from backswing to downswing is known as the transition. This move must be made correctly, and with a good tempo, to enable you to consistently strike the ball. At the top of the backswing, the shoulders should have turned through 90 degrees to the right, and your hips only 45 degrees. This has the effect of coiling or "winding up" the top half of your body against the lower half. The transition from backswing to downswing should almost happen automatically, appearing to be one continuous motion.

When you watch a good golf player, the transition appears as one move, but for the purpose of learning the correct moves, you should first try and feel it as a set of completely separate motions. When you have learned each of the steps below in sequence, you can then try and put it all into practice as a complete motion.

❶ At the top of the backswing you should feel your weight shifting onto the back foot.
❷ As you start the downswing, try and feel that your rear elbow is moving down to a position very close to your rear hip.
❸ Practise this feeling over and over again. Do it in slow motion, and really try to feel the correct sequence.

Feel your rear elbow move down toward your hip (see step 2).

Here we can see the rear elbow "tucked in" (see step 2).

THROWING PRACTICE

❶ A good practice exercise to help give you the feeling for the change of direction is to throw a ball. Next time you are on the practice ground, pick up a golf ball and throw it over arm (that is, with a straight arm), using a little bit of effort. ❷ You should really be able to feel your weight moving from your back foot to your front foot as you go from winding up your throwing arm to actually throwing the ball. Do this a few times, and then make some swings, trying to feel your body moving in the same fashion.

The main thing that can go wrong with this part of the swing, and one that very often does for the average golfer, is to start the downswing with the upper body. This is called "hitting from the top" and it can be very destructive for your shot. If this happens, the back shoulder "comes away" from the body as you make the transition, and this in turn will make you swing across the line of the ball. To avoid this, make sure that you keep the change of direction as smooth as possible. Remember – we are making a golf swing, so you must avoid the temptation to "hit" the ball.

TRANSITION TIPS

- Feel your weight shift to your back foot.
- Let your rear elbow move down towards your rear hip.
- Keep the movement smooth and unhurried.
- Avoid trying to "hit" the ball.
- Feel as if you are striking "through" the ball.

Keep the feeling of swinging through the ball rather than hitting it and you will play many more good shots.

Before you throw the ball, your weight is on the back foot ...

... which shifts to the front foot as your throw it (see step 2).

DOWNSWING TO IMPACT

If you have practised the transition from pages 44–45, you will now be a long way toward making your downswing and heading for a good impact position with the ball. It is important to remember that all these movements happen in a relatively short space of time, so you can't think of them all during your swing. Remember, a good player isn't thinking about his or her swing when striking the ball. To ensure you body builds up the memory of each element of the swing, it is important to practise each of the movements separately before trying to put the whole swing together.

Let's now look in detail at what happens from when you start your downswing to when you actually strike the ball.

❶ At the top of your backswing, your weight should have shifted to the back foot, and your rear elbow should have moved down close to your rear hip. During the course of your downswing, you need a feeling of driving your rear leg forward as you turn your body toward the target. The hands and arms should be swinging free and hard toward the ball.

❷ At impact, about 90% of your body weight will have shifted to your front foot, your hips will have turned past the ball, and your arms will have straightened.

During the course of the downswing your hands and arms should swing freely (see step 1).

At impact about 90% of your weight will shift to the front foot (see step 2).

Hands and arms should be at the set up position on impact (see step 3).

❸ Aim to return your hands and arms to their set up position when you reach impact. By turning your hips past the ball, you will have made space for your arms to swing through.

❹ You should be balanced, and you should feel that you are swinging toward the target. You should sweep the ball away at the bottom of your swing. Do not feel that you are hitting at the ball – just let the ball get in the way of your swing.

As mentioned previously, the main error you can make with the downswing is to start the movement with your upper body, which allows the back shoulder to come away from the body and as a result makes you swing across the line of the ball. To prevent this from happening, try to keep the change of direction as smooth as possible, and avoid actually "hitting" the ball.

DOWNSWING TIPS

• Drive the rear leg forward.

• Turn your hips toward the target.

• Let your hands and arms swing toward the target.

• Swing through the ball, don't hit at it.

Turning your hips allows your hands and arms to swing through (see step 3).

Feel your body turning toward the target as you swing through (see step 4).

The momentum of the swing will force your weight to the left at impact.

THE FOLLOW THROUGH

Even though you have now made contact with the ball, it is vital to continue your swing into a well-balanced, full follow through position. Take the opportunity to watch good golfers play and you'll notice that while there are many different types of swing, depending on factors such as height and build, they all finish in a very similar position. A well-balanced, full follow through is a sign of a well-balanced swing made with good rhythm and tempo. Working on this will really help you with every swing you make.

The following steps outline what to consider and how to practise completing your swing with what is known as the follow through.

❶ At the end of your swing you should feel that all your weight has shifted to your front foot, and you should be up on your back toe. A good way to practise this sensation is to make some swings with the thought that you are going to

At the end of the swing all your weight should be on the front foot (see step 1).

Show the spikes on the shoe of your back foot (see step 1).

Your hands should finish above your front shoulder (see step 3).

show the spikes on the sole of your rear shoe to someone standing behind you. If you do this it will really help you get your weight on to the front foot.

❷ If you get your legs working correctly as described above, you will turn your body through the ball. At the end of the swing, a good image for you to have is that you are trying to get your navel to point toward the target, or even slightly to the left. This will really encourage you to clear your hips out of the way, which allows you to swing through freely.

❸ Your hands and arms should freely swing all the way through, and your hands should finish above your front shoulder.

❹ When practising your swing, imagine a photographer taking pictures of you. He wants you to swing through to a full finish, and then hold the pose while he takes the photo. Learn to hold your finish like this, and it will ensure that you are swinging with a good rhythm and balance.

FOLLOW THROUGH TIPS

• Ensure your weight is completely on your front foot.

• Imagine that you are showing the spikes of your rear shoe to someone standing behind you.

• Your navel should be pointing toward the target.

• Your hands should be high over your front shoulder.

Remember to "hold the pose" at the end of the follow through (see step 4).

Make sure you are up on your rear toe ...

... and keep your hands raised high above your front shoulder.

SWING IN STAGES DRILL

Different people learn in different ways. Some learn by hearing, some learn by reading, and with golf, a lot of people find the best way to learn is by "feeling" the correct movements and motion of the swing. It is difficult to teach someone a feeling, but practice drills that break the swing into small sections help you to learn the correct sensation. Try to practise the drills over the next few pages repeatedly until they become second nature. If you can learn the correct sensations of the swing on the practice ground, it makes it much easier when you go out to play. You can then relax and trust the feelings of the swing that you have learned.

Swing in stages is a drill you can practise anywhere; you don't even need to hit balls. It is a great way of learning how to put each of the swing stages that you have learned into one complete swing.

The idea is to make each stage of the swing, and then briefly stop before moving onto the next section. If you practise this in front of a mirror, it is even more beneficial, as you can see as well as feel what is happening in your swing.

❶ Take your set up as usual.
❷ Make the takeaway part of the swing to halfway back and then stop. Check your position. Your weight should have shifted to the back foot; the shaft should be parallel to the ground, and also parallel to your toe line.
❸ Continue from there to the top of the backswing. Again, stop and check your position. Your shoulders should have turned through 90 degrees, 90% of your weight should be on your back foot, and your front arm will be comfortably straight.

Ensure you have a relaxed and comfortable set up (see step 1).

Check your halfway back position (see step 2).

Hold after the follow through (see step 6).

SWING IN STAGES TIPS

- Break the swing down into discrete stages.

- Practise each stage over and over again to really feel the sensation of each stage.

❹ The next move is the transition. Feel the weight shift back to the front, and the rear elbow move close to the rear hip. Stop and check this position.

❺ Swing down to impact. Check that your weight is on your front foot, your hips have cleared, and your arms have returned to the set up position.

❻ Swing through to the full follow through. Hold the position and check that your weight is completely on your front side, you are up on your rear toe, your navel is pointing toward the target, and you are completely balanced.

Do this drill very slowly, over and over again. After every fifth swing, stop and make two or three full-pace swings. With practice, you will learn the correct sensations of the swing.

Assess the position of your shoulders (see step 3).

Feel the rear elbow move down (see step 4).

Check your weight at impact (see step 5).

TOE TO THE SKY DRILL

This exercise is great for beginners learning to make their first swings. In fact, if you are learning golf for the first time, this is a perfect place to start, once you have mastered the set up. It also helps more experienced players feel two really important positions in the swing.

If you prefer, first set up some clubs on the ground as described in the Alignment Practice Drill on page 34.

❶ Tee up a ball on a low tee, and set up using a 6- or 7-iron.
❷ Now swing halfway back (waist high). There are four check points for you to look at to make sure you are swinging correctly: When the shaft is parallel to the ground, it should be parallel to the club laid on the floor along your toe line. The toe of the golf club should point to the sky. The grip end of the club should be roughly pointed at your navel. Your weight will be favouring your back foot.
❸ Now swing halfway through, and try to clip the ball away as you swing through. This is an easy swing, and the shots should not be going much more than 60yds (55m).
❹ When you make your swing, hold the finish, and again check the following four points: when the shaft is parallel to

the ground, it should point toward the target; the toe of the club should point to the sky; the grip end of the club should still be roughly pointed at your navel; and your weight will be favouring your front foot.

This drill may feel slightly stiff and wooden, but keeping the feeling that the grip end of the club is constantly pointing at your navel is a great way of feeling the vital connection between the arms and the body.

Even though this is a small swing, it is essential to feel that your weight moves to the rear foot on the backswing, and through to the front foot on the downswing.

Use a low tee and a 6- or 7-iron (see step 1).

Swing to the halfway back position (see step 2).

TOE TO THE SKY TIPS

- Get a real sense of your weight shifting to the rear foot on the backswing and to the front foot on the downswing.

- Check in which direction the toe of the club is pointing, both at backswing and follow through.

- Ensure the shaft is parallel to the ground at the finish.

Check the toe of the club is pointing toward the sky (see step 4).

Feel the weight shifting to the front foot as you swing (see step 3).

Check your position at the end of the stroke (see step 4).

FEET TOGETHER DRILL

This drill is useful for beginners and more experienced golfers alike. It will give you a really good feeling of how the arms should swing freely through the ball. Another of its benefits is that it will give you a great sense of rhythm and balance. If you swing too hard you will lose balance due to the fact that you have less of a foundation than with your normal stance.

❶ Place the ball on a low tee to start with. As you gain more confidence, you can take the tee away and hit the ball from the turf.

❷ Set up to the ball as normal, but then close your stance so that your feet are literally together.

❸ Make some swings with the feeling that you are really swinging within yourself. Try and clip the ball away with a free-flowing swing. If you start to lose balance, you are probably trying to hit the ball too hard.

❹ Once you become used to this drill, you will be amazed at how well you can strike the ball and how far you can hit it with so little effort.

This is a drill that you should go back to and use over and over again. Whenever your game is not as good as it should be, this is a way of getting you back on track. If this is the case, try hitting ten shots with your feet together, then ten normal shots, then ten with your feet together, and so on.

Take up your normal set up position, and then close your feet (see step 2).

Swing at the ball, ensuring that you don't lose your balance (see step 3).

With practice you'll find that you're able to hit the ball a surprisingly long way (see step 4).

THE BASEBALL SWING DRILL

The majority of golfers swing down and across the ball from outside the ball-to-target line. This creates many problems, the most common of which is a "slice", when the ball curves dramatically from left to right (or from right to left if you're a left-handed player).

Try the drill below and it will really help you to get the correct feeling of attacking the ball from inside the ball-to-target line.

❶ Take your set up as normal, then stand up to your full height and hold the club in front of you. It should be parallel to the ground at approximately waist height.
❷ Make some swings as if you were trying to hit a baseball. Another visual image that you can use is to imagine that you are hitting a ball off a tee that is 3ft (90cm) tall.
❸ This will force you to swing the club around your body, which will give you the feeling of the body and arms turning back and through together, and it will also force you to swing from the inside.
Repeat this exercise five times.

❹ Next, bend over slightly and imagine that you have the ball on a tee about 18in (45cm) high. Make five more swings with the thought of hitting the imaginary ball from the tee.
❺ Finally, try and hit five shots from a low tee. Hopefully the feelings that you developed with the practice swings – of swinging from the inside – will take over, and you will start to make much better contact with the ball.

Repeat this drill as and when you feel that you are swinging across the line of the ball.

Hold the club at waist height and parallel to the ground (see step 1).

Now make some swings as if you were using a baseball bat (see step 2).

Next, bend over slightly as if you were hitting the ball a little lower (see step 4).

PUMP AND SWING DRILL

Many golfers have great difficulty making the transition move in the swing. The move from backswing to downswing is critical, and the drill below is designed to help you get the correct feeling.

The most common mistake in this part of the swing is when the back arm separates from the body as you start down. It leads to hitting from the top and swinging across the line of the ball. To help try and stop this, use the following drill.

❶ Set up as normal, swing to the top of your backswing and then stop.
❷ From this point you need to try and feel a pumping motion of the rear arm. Feel like you are pumping your rear elbow down toward your rear hip. Stop, and swing back up to the top.
❸ Repeat this move three or four times and then go ahead and swing right through to the finish.
❹ If you are a beginner, to start with, you should try this

without the ball. More experienced players can go ahead and hit balls with this drill.

Remember, this is only a practice drill – it is not easy to make good contact with the ball, so don't worry too much about where it goes.

Once you have tried the drill a few times, try and make a few full swings without stopping. Hopefully, "muscle memory" or a more automatic reaction will take over, and you will make the transition move smoothly.

Stop at the top of the backswing (see step 1).

Pump the rear elbow down toward your rear hip (see step 2).

STOP AT THE TOP DRILL

This is another drill aimed at helping you avoid hitting from the top and swinging too hard at the ball. It is the perfect drill to help develop a good feeling of swinging the club at the ball rather than hitting at it.

It is very common, especially with the longer clubs, to find yourself hitting at or lunging at the ball. If this sounds familiar, you should try this simple drill.

❶ Tee up a ball and take your normal set up with an iron.
❷ Swing to the top of your backswing, pause for one second, and then swing down and sweep the ball away.
❸ Try to feel that you start the downswing slowly, and then accelerate the club through the hitting area.
❹ Swing through to your full-balanced finish position.
❺ Repeat this a few times until you really start to get the feeling of swinging down and through the ball rather than hitting at it.

Employing a short pause at the top of the backswing allows you time to gather all of your moving parts together in readiness for the downswing. It is so beneficial that there are many good players who actually use a small pause at the top during their actual swing.

Try it for yourself, and you will definitely get a better sense of timing and swing.

Pause at the top of the backswing for one second (see step 2).

Accelerate the club down to the hitting area (see step 3).

PUTTING

PUTTING

It may be surprising to devote an entire chapter to putting, but it is the most important shot in the game. A good putter will always beat someone who hits the ball well but putts badly. If a good player shoots a score of 70 for 18 holes, approximately 30 of these will be putts. An average player shooting a score of 100 will have approximately 42 putts. Therefore, whatever your standard, over 40% of shots are played with the putter. It's no surprise then that learning to putt well will really help improve your game.

Putting is often described as a game within a game, and this is quite a good description, because while there are similarities between the full swing and the putting stroke, there are also many differences. The main difference is that putting is the only shot in golf where we neither want nor need to add any loft to the shot.

As we go through the chapter, you will see that the grip and set up for putting are different from that of the full swing. However, both are equally as important and, once again, you really should learn to set up correctly before attempting to putt.

The actual act of striking the ball with a putter is called the putting stroke. Get the feeling of "stroking" the ball toward the hole rather than hitting or jabbing at it. There are two important factors that go into making a good putt.

The first is pace, the second is direction. It may sound strange, but pace is much more important than direction. When you first try putting, finding more or less the right direction is relatively easy, but judging the pace is a lot harder. There are various factors that make judging the pace difficult. These include whether the putt is uphill or downhill, whether the green is wet or dry, how long the grass is, and so on. If you can learn to take these various factors into account and learn how to judge the pace well, then you can be a great putter.

The putting stroke is the most important shot in the game.

Learning to putt well will take a great number of shots off your handicap.

PUTTING TIPS

- Learn to stroke the ball with the putter rather than hit it.

- The putting set up is just as important as the set up for any other shot.

- Learning to judge the pace of the putt is much harder and much more important than gauging direction.

- Learn to time your putting stroke as with all golf shots.

Putting is all about judging pace first and then direction.

PUTTING SET UP

As with any other golf shot, ensuring that you have the correct set up is essential for a good putting stroke. If your set up is incorrect, you're unlikely to be able to control the pace of the ball and strike it exactly in the direction you want. Over the next few pages we're going to apply the principles of GASPS to help you achieve the best putting set up – this should help you to remember how to go about preparing to make a putt when out on the course.

GRIP

The first difference you will notice about the putter is that the grip is not completely round like it is for all other clubs. There is a flat front that lines up square to the face of the putter. There are many different ways to grip the putter, but it is essential that you make sure that your thumbs are resting on the flat part of the grip.

The reverse overlap is the most common way that good players hold the putter, and it is a good place for you to start:

❶ Put the top, or leading, hand (left for right-handers, right for left-handers) at the top of the grip, with the thumb of your top hand pointing straight down the middle on the flat front of the grip. Then put your bottom hand on the club straight underneath the top, again ensuring that the thumb of your bottom hand points down the middle of the grip.

❷ To join your hands together, take the forefinger of the top hand off the grip, close up the gap that has now formed between the hands, and rest the forefinger of the top hand over the little finger of your bottom hand.

GRIP

A putter's grip is not exactly round.

Point the top thumb down the club (see step 1).

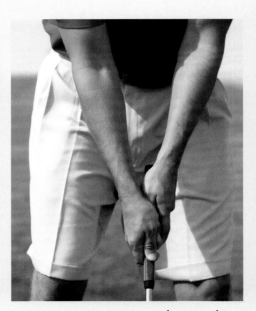

Add the bottom hand to the grip (see step 2).

AIM AND ALIGNMENT

Not all putts are straight, but for the purpose of learning the set up, presume that they are.

❶ Place the putter behind the ball, making sure that the face of the putter aims directly at the hole.

❷ As with the full swing, your feet, knees, hips, and shoulders should all be aligned slightly to the left, but parallel to an imaginary line drawn between the ball and the hole.

STANCE

The putting stance is an area where professional golfers display their individuality. But the main aim is to be comfortable over the ball, with eyes directly over it in order to make a confident putt.

❶ Set your feet slightly narrower than for the full swing – just inside your normal shoulder width set up position.

❷ Your weight should slightly favour your front side, with about 55% of your weight on your front foot.

❸ Place the ball just forward of centre in your stance – the idea being that you will stroke it slightly "on the up" as you go through.

POSTURE AND BALL POSITION

Many golfers make sure that everything is absolutely square to the ball and the line of putt – from the feet up to the shoulders. The arms should hang naturally.

❶ Bend forward from the waist, and try to feel that your arms are hanging comfortably, straight down from your shoulders.

❷ It is important to try and keep tension out of your body, because it will lead to a jerky stroke, so just let your knees gently flex and soften a little.

❸ It's also important when putting to try and get your eyes directly over the top of the ball so that you get the correct view of the putting line.

Practise the putting set up in front of a mirror, and get as comfortable as possible before attempting to hit some putts on the course.

AIM & ALIGNMENT

Aim the putter at the hole (see step 1).

STANCE

Place the ball just forward of centre (see step 3).

POSTURE

Gently flex your knees (see step 2).

THE PUTTING STROKE

The aim of the putting stroke is to swing the putter back and through so that the middle of the putter face meets the middle of the golf ball, with the putter face square to the line of the putt at impact. The putting stroke should be a smooth, fluid movement of the shoulders, hands, and arms. The rest of the body should stay as still as possible. Take a moment to consider the pendulum on an old grandfather clock. It swings back and forth at the same pace with a precise rhythm – tick-tock, tick-tock.

The pendulum is a great picture to have in your mind as you make your putting stroke. Just as it swings from the top of the clock, so too do you need to swing the putter from the top of your torso, in other words, from your shoulders. If you can get your shoulders to rock back and through, and let this gentle rocking motion lead your arms, hands, and the putter back and through, then you are well on your way to becoming a good putter. Bad putters generally use too much hand and wrist action in a stroke. As the hands and wrists have quite small muscles, they are much harder to control than the bigger muscles of the shoulders.

Set up as described on pages 62–63 and then stroke some putts with the grandfather clock image in your mind. To achieve a good putting stroke, use the following checklist:

❶ The backswing and through swing should be approximately the same length.
❷ The stroke should have a fairly consistent tempo, with just a slight acceleration into impact.
❸ The stroke should come from the shoulders, and not from the hands.
❹ The hands and wrists should be kept quite soft and relaxed, but do not let them become involved in the stroke.
❺ Your arms and the putter will form the letter Y. As you make your stroke, try and feel that the Y rocks back and through, and does not break down.
❻ The body should stay very still throughout the stroke.
❼ Keep your head still and do not look up until the ball is well on its way.

Take up the set up position as described on pages 62–63.

Make the back and through swing about the same length (see step 1).

Accelerate the club slightly at impact (see step 2).

Strike from the shoulders not from the hands (see step 3).

Your arms and putter should form the letter Y (see step 5).

Stay still during the stroke (see step 6).

Don't look up until after you've struck the ball (see step 7).

CHECK YOUR BALL POSITION DRILL

As we have seen, putting is a game within a game. Because of its importance in playing the game well and as a means of quickly improving your score, there are many practice drills that have been invented over the years. In the set up section of the putting chapter, you learned that in a good set up your eyes should lie directly over the top of the ball.

The following drill is a good way of checking to see if you have achieved this.

❶ Take up your putting set up position as described on pages 62–63.
❷ Next, staying as still as possible, take your bottom hand off the putter and take hold of a golf ball. (Have one in your pocket ready.)
❸ Hold the ball at the top of your nose, directly between your eyes.

❹ Let go of the ball, and let it fall to the ground. If your eyes are set up directly over the putting ball, the ball that you have dropped will hit it when it lands.
❺ If the ball does not hit the ball on the ground, try and see where it does contact the ground – this will help you adjust the putting ball into the correct position.

Repeat this exercise fairly regularly. If you can set up with your eyes over the ball every time it really will help you with your putting.

Hold a golf ball with your bottom hand at the top of your nose, between your eyes (see step 3).

Keeping your head as still as possible, drop the ball (see step 4).

If the dropped ball doesn't fall on the ball on the ground, adjust your position (see step 5).

Having your eyes directly over the ball will help your putting.

ROUND THE CLOCK DRILL

Holing short putts consistently can be a real confidence booster. It takes a lot of pressure off your long putting as well, because you won't mind hitting the ball past the hole if you know that you will hole the next one. Here are some short putt drills to practise.

Phil Mickelson, who is widely regarded as one of the best putters in the world, uses this drill – even on the course you sometimes see him rehearsing it.

❶ Go to the practice putting green and find a hole with a bit of slope around it.
❷ Spread six balls out around the hole at a distance of a approximately the length of a putter.
❸ Try to hole each of the putts in sequence around the hole.

If you hole every one, move a foot further away and repeat the exercise. It is important to add competitive pressure to your practice sessions – should you miss a putt, start all over again. Keep trying this until you hole 12 putts in a row. You will be surprised how much pressure you start to feel when standing over the 11th and 12th putts. This pressure replicates what you feel on the course when you are standing over an important putt, so it really is a great drill.

Place balls a putter's length from the hole (see step 2).

Hole each putt in sequence (see step 3).

TEE IN THE HOLE DRILL

It is very important to be positive when hitting short putts. Putts inside 4ft (1.2m) are often missed because they have not been hit firmly enough, which means the ball is more likely to be deflected by imperfections on the surface of the green.

This simple drill was designed to help you avoid the feeling of dribbling the ball to the hole, and help you to get the feeling of stroking it positively into the back of the hole.

❶ Go to the putting green and find a relatively flat putt.
❷ Put a tee peg right in the middle of the back of the hole, horizontally, so that it protrudes back into the hole.
❸ Hit three putts from 2ft (60cm) away. Be nice and positive and try to get the ball to make contact with the tee in the back of the hole.

❹ After you've tried from 2ft (60cm), move back to 3ft (90cm) and repeat the exercise, and then from 4ft (1.2m).

By practising this drill you really are teaching yourself to be positive with short putts, which is a surefire way of not missing them. When you go to play, try to visualise the tee in the back of the hole, and it will really help you to knock in those tricky short putts.

Place a tee peg in the middle of the back of the hole (see step 2).

Attempt to hit the tee peg with every putt (see step 3).

CLUB ON THE GROUND DRILL

Trying to be positive with your putts is just as important with long putts as it is with short ones. You should always try to get the ball past the hole when putting. There are two reasons for this. First, a ball that does not reach the hole has no chance of going in. Hit it hard enough and there is always the possibility that the hole will get in the way.

Second, if the ball runs past the hole you can watch it roll, and it will give you an idea of what the break will be on the second or "return" putt – this will help you to hole it.

However, you don't want to be too aggressive, otherwise you'll run the ball so far past the hole that you are constantly missing the return putts.

Practise the following drill to help you get the correct feeling of being positive without being overly aggressive.
❶ Go to the putting green, and place a club on the ground 2ft (60cm) behind the hole.
❷ Take five balls and move 15ft (4.5m) away from the hole. The idea is to hit the putts so that, if they do miss the

hole, they finish somewhere between the back of the hole and the club on the ground.
❸ Keep trying until you have successfully done this with all five balls. Now move back to 20ft (6m) and start all over again. When you have done it from this distance, move back to 25ft (7.5m), and so on.

Practising this drill will help you become more positive with your long putts, which will help you hole more, and also help reduce the number of three putts that you have.

Place a club 2ft (60cm) behind the hole (see step 1).

Ensure any missed putts stop between the hole and the club (see step 2).

PACE IS EVERYTHING DRILL

Good pace on your putts is vital. Most three putts are due to poor pace on long putts rather than poor direction. To become a good putter, it is vital that you manage to leave your long putts close to the hole, which then makes your next putt much easier. Developing "feel" for the longer putts is very important.

The following drill is designed to help you learn the feeling of pace. Practise it often enough and you really will start to develop the feel required to putt well.

❶ Find a fairly large practice putting green, ideally with a bit of a slope to it.
❷ Place nine balls around the edge of the green, spreading them out as much as possible.
❸ Stand in the middle of the green with nine balls. Stroke one putt at a time to each of the balls, trying to judge the pace of the putt as accurately as you can.

❹ Repeat the drill two or three times. Take your time between each putt, asking yourself: "Is the putt uphill, downhill, or fairly flat?" Take this information into account before you stroke the putt.

This is a great drill to practise just before you go out to play a round, because it will develop your feel for the green on that particular day.

Place balls around the edge of the green (see step 2).

From the centre of the green, putt out to each ball (see step 3).

CHANGE YOUR GRIP

Over the years there have been many different methods and ways for people to putt. However, most professionals and top players now agree that there are a few basic fundamentals and ideas that all good putters follow.

These fundamentals have been described at the start of this chapter, and include having your eyes over the ball, keeping your head and body still, and keeping your wrists out of the stroke as much as possible.

Despite these key fundamentals, there are a variety of different putting grips that people use, often in desperation, but often as a way of trying to improve the basics that they already have.

Here you will find a couple of variations on the standard grip that you learned in the putting set up section. If you are happy with that grip, and your putting is good, then skip this section. If, however you feel that there is room for improvement with your putting, try one or all of the following grips, and experiment to see what works for you.

TOP BELOW BOTTOM

One of the best players of all time, Jack Nicklaus, has stated that if he was learning golf for the first time, he would start with this putting grip. It helps to keep your shoulders level, and it is also very important to keep the back of the left (or right for left-handers) wrist firm.

❶ Put your right (left for left-handers) hand at the top of the grip, making sure that your thumb is pointing down the middle of the grip as normal.
❷ Next, put your other hand on the grip directly below the top hand. Again, ensure that your thumb points down the middle of the grip. Your hands will feel completely the wrong way round. Don't worry. Take the forefinger of

TOP BELOW BOTTOM

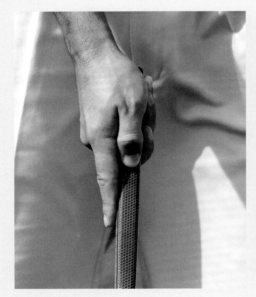

Place your right (right-handers)/left (left-handers) hand at the top (see step 1).

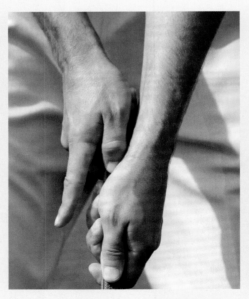

Place your other hand below the top hand and take your top forefinger off the club (see step 2).

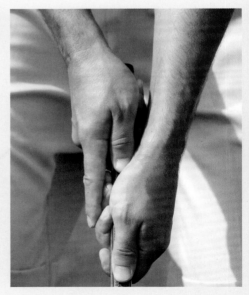

Rest the top forefinger over the fingers of the bottom hand (see step 3).

your top hand off the grip, and close up the space that it leaves between your hands.

❸ Rest the forefinger of your top hand down the outside of the fingers on the bottom hand.

Hit some putts with this method and see what happens. It is especially good from short range, because it stops the back of the bottom wrist from breaking down during the stroke.

THE CLAW

This grip is a fairly recent addition to the game. It will also feel a little strange to start with, but it's worth sticking with for a while in order to give it a proper try.

❶ Take the grip with your left (right for left-handers) hand at the top of the grip, making sure your left thumb is pointing straight down the middle.

❷ Place your other hand underneath the top hand, and grip the putter between your thumb and finger as though you were holding a pen. The palm of your bottom hand should be parallel to the putter face.

If you are struggling with your putting, try one of these grips. You might be pleasantly surprised.

A good standard grip is fundamental to your putting technique.

THE CLAW

Place your left hand (right for left-handers) at the top of the grip as normal (see step 1).

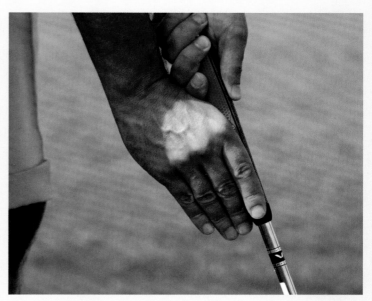

Take the grip between the thumb and forefinger of the bottom hand (see step 2).

READING THE GREENS

No matter how good your putting stroke is, it will not do you any good if you can't "read" the greens well. You need to be able to accurately assess if you're putting uphill, downhill, and if the ball will move either from left-to-right or right-to-left. There are many factors to take into account when attempting to read a green. If you can learn to do it well, it will prove invaluable throughout your golfing career, and your score will improve dramatically.

Follow the ideas below, and you will become proficient at reading the greens.

• You should start to read the green as you walk up to it. Take into account the general lie of the land. Ask yourself where the predominant slopes are. There is quite a good chance that the lie of the land will affect the general slope of the green, and therefore your putt.

• Have a look for any water such as a pond, a lake, or river. With very few exceptions, putts tend to break toward the water, so if the water is on the left of the green, the ball will tend to break to the left, and vice versa.

• Check if the green is wet or dry. This will have a big effect on how much a ball will break. If the green is dry, your putts will break much more than if it is wet. This can change during the course of your round. If you tee off early in the morning, there may well be dew on the greens when you start, which will dry out as you play. If you play in the evening, dew can start to settle toward the end of the round. Check it on every green.

• Once you are on the green, stand directly behind the ball, in line with the hole, and crouch down as low as you can get. This is the most important view and you should be able to see whether the green slopes left-to-right, or right-to-left.

• Walk to a spot halfway between the ball and the hole, and a little way to the side of the line of the putt. Again, crouch down and from this angle you will be able to judge whether the putt is uphill or downhill.

Crouching behind the ball provides the best view.

Assess whether the putt is uphill or downhill.

• If you are happy that you have enough information to make your putt, then go ahead and hit it – if not, go and stand behind the hole, crouch down and look at the putt from a reverse angle. This alternative view can sometimes give you a different perspective, which will hopefully confirm your original thoughts.

• On very long putts, break the putt up into two sections in your mind. Remember the ball will break more in the second half of the putt as the ball loses pace.

• Never hit your putt until you are as confident as you can be that you know what the break is. Do not guess.

No one gets it right every time. However, if you follow these guidelines before you putt on every green, you can be sure to give yourself the best possible chance of hitting a good putt.

Never guess which way the ball will break.

A reverse angle of the putt can often reinforce your assessment of the shot.

THE
SHORT GAME

THE SHORT GAME

The short game is a collective term given to all golf strokes that require you to hit a shot a distance that is less than a full wedge. For the majority of players, and for the purpose of this book, you can assume that all the shots covered in this section are less than 100 yards (90m) long – in fact, the majority of them will be less than 50 yards (45m). As with putting, the short game is often overlooked on the practice ground – but build up your confidence in your short game and you'll quickly see your scores begin to drop.

Whatever standard of golf you've reached, approximately 60% of all your shots will be played within 100yds (90m) of the flag. We have already discovered that around 40% of the game is played on the greens, so that still leaves 20% of the game to be played inside 100yds (90m) before you reach the green.

These shots can be difficult because they require less than a full swing, and that magic word "feel" comes into play again – you have to feel how hard to hit each shot. The good news is that feel is something you can develop with practice.

To try and get an understanding of feel, imagine you have a ball in your hand and you are trying to roll it 10yds (10m). If you are standing on tarmac it will require very little power to get the ball to roll 10yds (10m). However, if you are standing in grass that is 3in (7cm) long, it will require quite a lot of power to make the ball go   (10m).

This is a very basic example, but all of us have an in-built element of feel already. As you know, you have to roll the ball harder through the grass than you would on the tarmac. That, in simple terms, is feel.

Practising your short game will pay dividends when you hit the course for real.

Starting with the chip and run, and moving on to pitching and bunker shots, throughout the course of this chapter you will learn the basic techniques of all the shots that you need to master the short game.

At the end of the chapter there are various drills and practice exercises that will help you to develop the techniques needed to master the short game, and just as importantly other drills that will help you to learn and develop feel for distance – essential for all short shots around the green.

If you develop a good short game, it really does make the rest of the game easier. Putting becomes easier because if you chip close you will be faced with shorter putts, and the long game becomes easier because if you are confident that you can chip close when you hit a bad approach shot, it really takes the pressure off.

Learn the techniques, then practise, practise, and practise some more!

Having a good feel for distance is essential for a successful short game.

THE CHIP AND RUN

The chip and run is a basic shot that can be used from when you're just off the green, but also from further away when there are no obstacles between you and the hole. The ball flies quite low to the ground, and then runs the remaining distance to the hole. As with all short game shots, having a good feel is paramount and will enable you to get the ball to roll up very close to the hole. This will allow you to finish with a single putt – getting "up and down" in two shots is a skill at which all professionals excel.

To play the shot, follow the GASPS sequence outlined here:

GRIP
This shot is about accuracy rather than distance. Because of that you should take your normal grip, and then move your hands down the club so that your top hand is positioned at the bottom of the grip on the club. This has the effect of shortening the club, giving you much greater control.

AIM AND ALIGNMENT
Aim the clubface in the direction that you want to hit the shot. You should align your feet a little to the left (or right for left-handers) of target so that your hips will start from a slightly open position. As you are not making a full swing, you will not be able to clear your hips, so starting with them slightly open allows you the freedom to swing the club toward the target.

STANCE AND BALL POSITION
Your feet should be positioned much closer together than for a full shot. This is something you can experiment with, but start with your heels about 10in (25cm) apart. The ball should be positioned back in your stance, and should be placed opposite your right heel. Your body weight should

GRIP

Move your hands down the club.

AIM AND STANCE

Aim the clubface at the target.

POSTURE

Keep your knees soft and relaxed.

favour the left side, with about 75% of your weight on your front foot. Your hands should also be forward, with the bottom hand opposite the inside of the front thigh. If you have set up correctly, your front arm and the club shaft should form a straight line.

POSTURE
Because you are gripping down the club, you will naturally be standing much closer to the ball than you would for a full shot. Your knees should be soft not tense, and your arms should hang comfortably straight down. As with all shots, try to feel relaxed during your set up.

SWIG
❶ Due to the set up position of the ball being back in the stance, and with your hands and weight forward in the stance, your hands will already be in a position where they are in front of the clubface and the ball.
❷ The swing for this shot is quite short – similar to a putting stroke – so play the shot with your hands staying in front of the clubhead at all times. As with the putt, your shoulders, arms, hands, and club all move back and through together.

CHIP AND RUN TIPS

• Hold the club lower down.

• Ensure you have nice soft knees.

• Hold your hands in front of the clubhead.

❸ Try to keep the line between the front arm and the club shaft in place throughout the stroke. Do not try and flick the ball into the air with your wrists. Let the loft on the club chip the ball up and forward.

Once you have learned the basic technique, practise chipping with various clubs – a 6-, 7-, 8-, or 9-iron, as well as with a wedge and sand wedge. Watch how the ball reacts differently with every club. To decide which club to use when, look at the Try Different Clubs Drill on pages 84–85.

SWING

Keep your hands ahead of the ball (see step 1).

Swing resembles a putting stroke (see step 2).

Let the club lift the ball (see step 3).

USE TWO CLUBS DRILL

A common mistake that people make when chipping is to use too much wrist action. To stop this, and to give you the correct feeling for the stroke, try the following drill. Try this and other practice drills over the next few pages to become confident with the feeling and technique of a good chip shot.

Before you start, think through a chip shot before executing it. This is essential if you want to hit chip shots consistently well – if you don't know where the ball will land, you are unlikely to get close to the hole.

❶ Take a wedge and a 9-iron. Grip the wedge as normal for a chip shot, then turn the 9-iron upside down and hold its handle next to the wedge so it forms one really long club.

❷ Take your chipping set up as normal so that the shaft of the 9-iron points to the left (or right for left-handers) of your body.
❸ From this position, hit some chip shots. If you use too much wrist action, the shaft of the 9-iron will hit the left (or right) side of your body.
❹ Keep practising until you can hit every chip correctly without too much wrist action.

Hold the two clubs together to form one long club (see step 1).

The shaft will run up the front side of your body (see step 2).

ROCK THE SHAFT DRILL

This exercise is intended to help you get the feeling of using the big muscles in your shoulders and arms to control the chip, rather than using your hands and wrists.

Another drill to improve your technique.

❶ Set up as normal to hit a chip shot, but hold the shaft of another club against your chest with your shoulders and arms. This shaft should be parallel to the ground.
❷ As you make the chip try and get a feeling of rocking the shaft up and down. Feel it go up on your rear side as you swing back, and then feel it go up on the front side as you swing through.

ROCK THE SHAFT TIPS

- Chip with your shoulders and arms.

- Try to really feel the shaft of the club rocking up and down as you swing.

- Swing like the pendulum of a clock.

Hold the club against your chest with your arms (see step 1).

Rock the shaft up and down (see step 2).

TRY DIFFERENT CLUBS DRILL

This next exercise will help you to learn how different clubs "behave" when used to play a chip shot. The first drill will familiarise you with how different clubs produce different results, and the second variation will give you an idea of which club you chip best with.

❶ Stand at the edge of the practice green with 18 balls. Hit three chip shots each with a 6-iron, a 7-iron, an 8-iron, a 9-iron, a pitching wedge, and finally with a sand wedge.
❷ Try to make the same swing with each shot – in other words, don't vary the strength of your swing. Watch how the balls react with each of the different clubs. You should notice that the 6-iron flies very low to the ground and then rolls a long way, and as you go through the clubs to the sand wedge you will notice how with each successive club the ball flies higher but rolls less.
❸ To start with, use the table to estimate how to judge the reaction of the ball on the green. This is based on an averagely paced, relatively flat green.

❹ Using the table below, if you are facing a chip shot of 10yds (10m) and you use the 7-iron, you need to strike the ball so that it carries 2½yds (2.5m) (25%) and it will then run 7½yds (7.5m) (75%). If you use a 9-iron you need to carry the ball 4yds (4m) (40%) and let it run 6yds (6m) (60%) With a sand wedge carry it 6yds (6m) (60%), and let it run 4yds (4m) (40%). This table is a good guide to use

Club	Carry (%)	Roll (%)
7-iron	25	75
9-iron	40	60
sand wedge	60	40

Begin with a 6-iron (see step 1).

Move through to an 8-iron (see step 1).

Also try out a sand wedge (see step 1).

when playing, but remember to take ground conditions and any slope on or around the green into account.

The following drill is an excellent variation of the first drill. It will help you develop feel, and it will give you an indication as to which club you chip best with.

❶ Position groups of three balls around the outside edge of the practice green in six different locations.

❷ Pick one of the holes on the green as a target. Take your 7-iron and go to each pile of balls chipping one from each pile toward your target. When you have done that, do exactly the same with a 9-iron, chipping one from each pile, and then do exactly the same with your sand wedge. Repeat the exercise two or three times, after which you should have an improved sense of how each club behaves differently and how you need to play the shot to get the same result – that is, to get as close to the hole as possible.

Using different clubs will help you feel how each behaves.

CHIP IT FURTHER DRILL

The aim of this drill is to refine your feel for the wedge, specifically in terms of how hard to swing the club to reach a certain distance. There are two variations of this drill: the first you can practise alone, the second with a friend.

The idea is to progressively chip each shot further than the one before:

❶ Go to the practice ground with your wedge and balls.
❷ Start by hitting a fairly short chip just a few yards. Then take another ball and try to chip it just a little further than the first one.
❸ Keep repeating this until you fail to hit a shot further than the one before – if you do, you have to start all over again. Keep a score of how many shots you can do in a row. Try to get to ten before you stop.

If you have a friend of a similar standard to yourself, it is a great idea to play practice games with them. Not only is this enjoyable, but it adds a much-needed competitive edge.

❶ Take it in turns to pick a chip shot, and play two balls each. Whoever hits it closest to the hole scores one point.
❷ Keep going until one of you reaches ten points and wins.

CHIP IT FURTHER TIPS

• Begin with a short shot.

• Try to feel the weight of each shot.

• Make the challenge important to you.

Hit each shot slightly further than the last (see step 2, first drill).

Try a little competitive practice with a friend (see step 1, second drill).

CHIP WITH A WOOD DRILL

Over the last few years, playing a chip shot with either a fairway wood or hybrid or rescue club has become increasingly popular with players of all levels. It can be used from various situations close to the green. For example, if your ball is sitting down in the semirough close to the green, or if you have a poor lie on the fairway, this can be a great way of an easy escape.

This should be played with a lofted wood such as a 5-wood, or a hybrid or rescue club.

❶ Take your putting grip and take hold of the club right at the bottom of the grip.

❷ Aim the clubface at the hole, but aim your feet a little to the left (or right for left-handers). Assume your normal chipping set up.

❸ Your feet should be close together, with approximately 60% of your body weight favouring the front foot. The ball should be positioned in the middle of your feet.

❹ Because the club is quite long, you need to stand up quite tall, or the top of the grip will snag in your clothing.

❺ Play the shot in a similar way to a putt. Feel the shoulders rock back and through and keep the wrist action to a minimum. Ensure the clubhead is very close to the ground throughout the swing. The ball should pop forward with very little loft, but will then run out very well. Feel as if you are hitting it about as hard as you would hit a putt from the same distance.

Practise it next time you are on the chipping green. Try it from various lies including the semirough and bad lies on the fairway. You will be surprised at how well this shot works.

Aim your feet slightly off to the left (see step 2).

Keep wrist action to a minimum (see step 5).

PITCHING

Pitching is a shot played with a wedge or sand wedge. It is generally used for longer distances than chipping, and also usually entails a higher shot than a chip and run. A pitch travels most of its distance in the air, and does not run very far after it lands. It is a term used to describe most shots played between 30 and 100 yards (27–90m). As with the chip and run, pitching consistently well will take pressure off having to make difficult long putts, and may occasionally save you a shot if you can get up and down in two.

Follow these steps to learn the basic pitching technique:

❶ With your normal grip, move down the club's grip slightly, for more control. How much to "grip down" depends on the length of shot that you are playing, and is something that comes with practice and experience. The shorter the shot, the further down the grip you should go.

❷ For a basic pitch shot, make sure that the clubface points directly at the target. As with the chipping set up, you should set up with your feet a little bit open (aligned to the left for right-handers, to the right for left). Again, this will help you to clear your hips at impact, because you will not

be making a full swing, and it will also help you to keep your back swing a little bit shorter and more under control.

❸ Your stance should be a little narrower than it would be for a full shot. Your weight should slightly favour your front side, with about 60% of your body weight on your front foot. The ball should be positioned in the middle of your feet for a standard pitch shot.

❹ Your posture should be very similar to the one you assume for a full swing. However, because we have choked down on the grip a little bit, you will automatically be

Grip down the club (see step 1).

Use a slightly open stance (see step 2).

Your stance is narrower than normal (see step 3).

standing a little bit closer to the ball, and therefore be more bent over than normal. This encourages a slightly steeper swing, which is perfect for pitching.

❺ The length of the swing will depend on the length of the shot you are hitting. This only comes with practice. Try to make the backswing the same length as the forward swing. Therefore, if you swing back to waist height, swing through to waist height. If you swing back to shoulder height then swing through to shoulder height. You should try and feel that you are hitting down slightly on the ball with a swing that is gently accelerating at impact. Do not try and lift the ball yourself – let the club lift it for you.

There are many different variations of the pitch shot. Once you have learned the technique above, move on to the short game drills on pages 90–93 to learn how to vary the distance and trajectory of your shots. Use a pitching wedge and practise pitching with a half-length swing, get used to the feeling, and then practise it with a three-quarter-length swing. If you can become competent with these two shots, it will make developing your pitching skills much easier.

Ensure that your body and arms work together.

Swing will be slightly steeper (see step 4).

Hit "down" slightly on the ball (see step 5).

Ensure an even follow through (see step 5).

USING A LOB WEDGE

Now you have learned the basic pitching technique it is important to practise short and long pitches to start and develop a feel for distance. If you follow the drills over the next few pages, you should really start to develop a good pitching technique and be able to adjust your stroke for every shot required.

This is not so much a drill as an invaluable tip. If you don't already have a lob wedge, you should seriously consider buying one. A lob wedge has 60 degrees of loft as opposed to a sand wedge, which has 54 degrees. The extra six degrees of loft really allows you to be positive with short pitches, so enabling you to get the ball to fly very high and therefore stop very quickly. A lob wedge takes some time to get used to, because you have to hit shots quite firmly to cover a short distance. However, if you buy one and then practise and persevere with it, you'll wonder how you ever coped without it.

The added loft on a lob wedge gets the ball to fly high and stop very quickly.

THE UMBRELLA DRILL

Take a bag of practice balls to the range, together with your wedges and an umbrella to hit shots into. This exercise is harder than you think, and if you're struggling to get three balls in the umbrella, start with two or even one.

❶ Open up the umbrella and spike it into the ground 30yds (27m) away. Keep hitting shots until you land three balls into the umbrella. Bouncing it in doesn't count!

❷ Once you have pitched three balls in, move the umbrella back a further 10yds (10m) to 40yds (36m) and repeat the exercise until you have again pitched three balls in.

❸ Repeat the exercise again from 50yds (45m).

As you build up your skill and confidence increase the amount of balls you need to hit into the umbrella before you move on.

The balls have to land directly in the umbrella – bouncing them in doesn't count!

THE CLOCK FACE DRILL

A common mistake with pitching is to decelerate the clubhead as it reaches the ball. This can be very destructive and will lead to poorly struck shots. A good way to alleviate this problem and to improve your feel is to use the Clock Face Drill. This visualization drill allows you to imagine the length of your swing in relation to a clock face.

❶ As you set up, imagine your head is at 12 o'clock and your club is at 6 o'clock. Try to match the length of your backswing to the length of your forward swing. Take five balls and swing back to 8 o'clock then swing through to 4 o'clock as you strike them.
❷ Repeat the exercise with another five balls, but this time swing back to 9 o'clock, then swing through to 3 o'clock as you strike them.
❸ Take another five balls and this time swing back to 10 o'clock, then swing through to 2 o'clock.
Using this visual image as you swing will help you to keep the backswing and the through swing the same distance. This is really important with pitching, because it allows you to keep a reasonably consistent tempo throughout the swing with a smooth acceleration into impact.

CLOCK FACE TIPS

• The backswing and follow through should be even.

• Accelerate through to impact.

Swing from 9 to 3 o'clock (see step 2).

Swing from 10 to 2 o'clock (see step 3).

Accelerate through the ball.

DISTANCES DRILL

This will be the best pitching tip you ever receive. It will allow you to be really precise with your pitching distances, and if you are precise with distance control, you will definitely improve your scores. Go to the practice ground on a day without much wind. Take your pitching wedge, sand wedge, and lob wedge, if you have one, together with a bag of balls, and a pen and paper.

Write down your average distances

After completing this drill, you should have a piece of paper that looks like this:

Club	1/2 swing	3/4 swing	Full swing
Pitching wedge	65yds (60m)	85yds (75m)	110yds (100m)
Sand wedge	55yds (50m)	75yds (70m)	100yds (90m)
Lob wedge	45yds (40m)	65yds (60m)	90yds (80m)

The yardages/meters used are for illustration purposes only; yours will obviously be a little different. The great thing with this is that when you go to play on the course, every time you are left with a tricky pitch shot, you can pace off the distance, and then see which shot from your chart gets you the closest result. This will give you the confidence needed to execute the shot well.

If you use this method then you only need to learn three swings. By using these three swings with three different clubs you are giving yourself nine different shots. Your accuracy and distance control will definitely improve.

Think back to the clock face drill (opposite), as you will need it for this exercise.

❶ Begin by hitting 15 balls with your pitching wedge, using a half swing. On the clock face, imagine swinging from 9 o'clock to 3 o'clock. When you have done this, pace out from where you hit the shots to the average distance of the 15 balls. Write down the distance.
❷ Repeat the exercise with your sand wedge and then your lob wedge, making sure that you write down the average distance each time.
❸ When you have done this, visualise a slightly longer swing, with the arms swinging back to 10 o'clock and through to 2 o'clock. This is a ¾ length swing. Hit 15 balls with each club, and again write down the average distance for each one.
❹ Finally, hit 15 balls with each club, making a full swing.

Get to learn you clubs' distances at set swings.

GREENSIDE BUNKER SHOTS

Most golfers dread facing a bunker shot. It can create fear in even the calmest of players. However, with the correct technique, the greenside bunker shot is actually one of the easiest shots in the game – watch the professionals and in the vast majority of cases they'll come out of the bunker first time, and not only that but nine times out of ten they'll leave themselves a relatively short putt to finish the hole. Sure they make it look easy, but in reality there's a large margin for error, because you don't even need to hit the ball!

To play out of sand traps with confidence every time, follow these GASPS tips.

GRIP

When playing out of a bunker, it's important to open the clubface in order to get extra loft on the shot, and also to allow the club to bounce through the sand. To do this you should turn the club to the right (or left for left-handers) so that the face is looking about 45 degrees to the right (or left) of where you want to go. Only when you've done this should you take your grip. You will actually be gripping the club to the left (or right) of centre. Do not make the mistake of gripping the club as normal and then opening the face. This will not work, because your hands will come back to their normal position when you swing, and the clubface will no longer be open. You should also choke down on the club and grip about 2in (5cm) further down than normal.

Open the clubface to gain extra loft.

Aim the clubface at the target.

AIM AND ALIGNMENT

If you set up as normal, the clubface will be pointing to the right (or left for left-handers) due to the open clubface, so it is vital that you shuffle around in the sand until the clubface is again pointing directly at the target. Your feet, knees, hips, and shoulders should now be pointing about 45 degrees to the left (or right) of the target.

STANCE AND BALL POSITION

Shuffle your feet into the sand about an inch (2.5cm). This is useful because it helps to give you a firm base in the loose sand, helps you test how hard or soft the sand is, and moves your body lower in the set up, which will help you hit the sand just behind the ball.

The ball should be positioned forward in your stance, and your body weight should slightly favour your front side, with about 60% of your weight on your front foot.

POSTURE

You need to get a sensation of "sitting in" to this shot. To do this, there will be more flex in your knees than for a normal shot. Try and get your knees to point to the left of the ball, which will help you to skim under the ball when you swing.

GREENSIDE BUNKER SHOT TIPS

- Open the clubface.

- Shuffle your feet in the sand.

- Feel the club bounce through the sand.

SWING

The bunker shot swing is like no other. Try to hit the sand about 2in (5cm) behind the ball, and then make a long follow through even though it is a short shot. The idea is to explode the sand out of the bunker, and let the ball float out with it. To do this you need to swing along the line of your feet (left – or right – of the target), and feel the club bounce through the sand.

Practise this shot over and over until you become confident that you can consistently make the correct swing. It will feel a little strange at first, because you are aiming and swinging off to where you want the ball to go. You must trust the open clubface to send the ball to your target.

The ball should be forward of centre.

Flex your knees more than for other shots.

BUNKER SHOT DRILLS

Now you have the basic idea of how to play a bunker shot, how do the pros make it look so easy? Practise the drills and exercises in this section and you'll start to see for yourself that it actually is a fairly simple shot.

DRAW YOUR SET UP

This exercise ensures that you swing away from the flight of the ball – to the left for right-handers, right for left-handers.

❶ Go into a practice bunker with a few balls. Put the first one down and pick up your sand wedge. Draw a line in the sand from the front of the ball for about 1yd (1m) in the direction that you want to hit the shot.
❷ Now draw a line just to the left of the ball, aiming 45 degrees to the left (or right for left-handers) of your target.
❸ When you set up, make sure to open the clubface, and set up parallel to the second line in the sand. As you swing, use this line as a visual image to help you swing away from the target. As long as you have kept the clubface open the ball will fly toward the flag.

DRAW AN IMPACT LINE

This is a great drill because it takes your focus away from the ball, and makes you concentrate on hitting the sand.

❶ Set up six balls in a line about 6in (15cm) apart in a greenside bunker. Then draw a line in the sand about 2in (5cm) behind the row of balls.
❷ Try to hit the balls out of the bunker using the standard greenside bunker shot technique. The idea is to impact the sand where the line is drawn. You can see how well you're doing because when your club strikes the sand it will leave a mark. Practise this repeatedly until you can hit the line every time.

When you next play out of a bunker, pretend this line is in the sand and it will help to ease the anxiety of the shot.

DRAW YOUR SET UP　　DRAW AN IMPACT LINE

A second line runs 45° from the first (see step 2).

Draw a line behind the balls (see step 1).

Hit the impact line behind the balls (see step 2).

SKIM A STONE

The correct action of the bunker shot is a feeling of swinging from out-to-in across your body with a positive acceleration under the ball. To create this feeling, imagine you are trying to skim a stone across a lake. To do this, your right (or left for left-handers) arm swings across your body as you try to start the stone flying on a fairly flat trajectory.

❶ Pick up your sand wedge in your bottom hand and make some one-handed swings in the bunker, trying to create the stone-skimming feeling in your bottom hand and arm.
❷ Try without the ball to start with, and once you get used to the feeling, try and do it with ball.

This will really help you to obtain the correct feeling of the bunker shot swing.

CHANGE THE DISTANCE

The shots you have been practising in this section are all concerned with bunkers close to the green. However, even in a greenside bunker you will need to vary the length of the shot, depending on where the flag is. The easiest way to achieve this is to vary the amount of sand that you take. In simple terms, the less sand that you take, the further the ball will go.

❶ To practise this, take a bag of balls into a practice bunker, and put six of them down in a line. Draw a line 2in (5cm) behind the balls and practise hitting them out as described earlier in the Draw An Impact Line Drill (opposite). See how far the balls travel, and if it helps you for later, write down the distance.
❷ Now put six more balls down in a line, but this time draw a line in the sand 3in (7.5cm) behind the balls. Again, hit all the balls out using the same swing as above. Because you are hitting an inch more of sand, the balls will travel a shorter distance. Once again, make a note of how far they have gone.
❸ Finally, place another six balls and draw a line in the sand 1in (2.5cm) behind them. Go through the same process again and these balls should fly a little further. Write down the distance traveled.

When you next go out to play, you'll have three different length bunker shots with one simple swing, giving you a really easy way to start to vary the distance of your greenside bunker shots. This will allow you to hit the ball closer much more often.

SKIM A STONE

CHANGE THE DISTANCE

Swing the club with one hand (see step 1).

Vary the distance of the impact line ...

and record how far each ball travels (see step 3).

THE PLUGGED BUNKER SHOT

The plugged bunker shot is one of the most feared shots in golf – particularly among weekend golfers. The plugged lie or "fried egg" occurs when the ball comes into the sand trap from a great height and partially buries itself. It has been the undoing of countless thousands of rounds of golf, single-handedly ruining a respectable-looking scorecard. This shot is played very differently than a normal bunker shot. Follow the instructions below and you'll find that it's possible to escape with only one or two shots dropped.

GRIP
Grip the club as normal but hold it a little tighter than usual, especially with your top hand. To hit the sand quite hard you must have a firm grip.

AIM AND ALIGNMENT
Unlike the normal bunker shot, you should set up with everything square. You don't need to open the clubface, so you don't have to open out the body. Take your normal square set up as you would for a full shot.

STANCE AND BALL POSITION
Your stance should be shoulder width apart, and your weight should be favouring the front side with approximately 75% of your body weight on your front foot. The ball should be positioned back in your stance, and should be to the right (or left for left-handers) of centre in your stance. By having your weight on the front foot and the ball set closer to your back leg, you are encouraging a steep swing, which is essential for this shot.

Grip the club tighter than usual.

Position the ball back in your stance.

POSTURE

Your posture should be as normal, but you should feel that you are leaning toward the hole due to your weight being over on your front foot.

SWING

When swinging, try to hinge your wrists very early in the backswing – you should feel as if you are swinging up a lot steeper than normal. Your weight should not shift back as it would in a normal swing, but must stay on your front foot. Focus on a spot 2in (5cm) behind the ball and swing the club down hard onto this spot.

You need to be very positive and hit it with a powerful descending blow. Due to the fact that you have swung down so sharply, you won't be able to follow through. The club should feel that it has become buried in the sand.

The ball will come out much lower than a normal bunker shot, and it will not stop very quickly. You have to allow for this low ball flight and lots of roll when you are trying to judge the shot. It is much harder to be accurate with this shot than it is with a normal bunker shot, so your main aim must be to get the ball out of the bunker and onto the green. Do not worry too much about getting the ball close to the hole – just try to get it on the green.

Practise this shot for 15 minutes and you will be amazed at how easy such a difficult looking shot can be.

Hit the ball with a powerful descending blow.

There should be little or no follow through.

THE MIDRANGE BUNKER SHOT

Widely regarded as the hardest shot in golf, even by the tour pros, the midrange bunker shot (approximately 40–60yds/35–55m) need not be as difficult as most people think. There are two different methods to use, depending on the situation and what other hazards lie between your ball and the hole. The first option, and definitely the easiest, can be used when there are no hazards. All you have to do is play a normal bunker shot, but instead of using a sand wedge, use a pitching wedge or even a 9-iron.

Using a steeper-lofted club, the ball will come out lower than normal, and carry and run a bit further compared with using a sand wedge. Try it with a pitching wedge and a 9-iron, and if there is not much lip on the bunker you can even try it with an 8-iron.

However, if there is a hazard between the ball and the hole, you'll have to try an alternative approach, which is more difficult but is designed to fly high and stop quickly.

To achieve this, the strike needs to be precise to get the correct distance. Follow the tips below, then practise them as much as possible.

GRIP
Take your normal grip with a sand wedge, open the face slightly, and choke down the club about an inch.

Open the clubface slightly.

The ball should lie forward of centre.

Stand slightly taller.

AIM AND ALIGNMENT

Stand slightly open (to the left of the target for right-handers, to the right for left-handers) with your feet, knees, hips, and shoulders. Keep the clubface pointing to the target.

STANCE AND BALL POSITION

Assume your normal bunker shot stance for this shot, but the ball should lie back toward the centre of the stance so that it is just forward of centre in your feet.

POSTURE

With the basic greenside bunker shot, you learned to sit down into the shot. With this midrange bunker shot, adopt a more standard posture so that you are standing slightly taller. You should have the same posture that you would have for a normal shot.

SWING

Try to swing along the line of your feet (slightly out-to-in), aiming to contact the sand much closer to the ball than with a normal bunker shot. You should be aiming to hit the sand about ½in (1.5cm) behind the ball. It is really important to be precise because if you hit too much sand the ball won't go far enough, and if you take too little sand you can send the ball flying over the green. Your swing should be about 3/4 length on both the backswing and through swing and, as usual, the club should be accelerating at impact.

This is quite a difficult shot that requires a great deal of practice. Spend some time in a practice bunker and really try to learn the correct impact position of just behind the ball. It is also important to feel the club skimming through the sand and not digging in.

Swing along the line of your feet (out-to-in).

Accelerate the club at impact.

Follow through with a 3/4 swing.

THE LOB SHOT

This is a spectacular-looking shot, but one that is very difficult to master. It is sometimes called the "parachute shot" because, played correctly, the ball floats up high and stops very quickly when it lands on the green. Sometimes the only way to get the ball close is to use this shot, for example if you have a bunker between you and the green, and the flag is close to the bunker so requiring you to stop the ball quickly. Many of the pros make this shot look easy, but you should only try it after you have put in a lot of practice.

The technique is similar to that of the greenside bunker shot, but because you are not hitting sand there is a lot less margin for error.

GRIP
Open the clubface as you did for the greenside bunker shot. Grip down the club a little to get more control.

AIM AND ALIGNMENT
Your clubface will be looking to the right (left for left-handers) of the target, so you need to move your alignment to the left (or to the right) until the club once again points at the target.

STANCE AND BALL POSITION
Your stance should be fairly wide, to give you a good base to swing from. Your weight should favour your front side, with 60% of your body weight on your front foot. The ball position should be forward of centre in your stance, depending on the lie. The better the lie you have the closer to the front foot you can position the ball.

Open the clubface before taking your grip.

Feel as if you're "sitting in" to the shot.

POSTURE

Try to "sit in" to the shot. Really soft knees will help give you the correct feel for this.

SWING

Make a positive swing along the line of your feet from out-to-in. Try to feel that you are cutting across the ball and sliding the club underneath it.

You must accelerate the club through impact or there will be disastrous results. Any sign of deceleration and the ball will go nowhere near far enough.

Hit it hard and trust the fact that the ball will go up and stop quickly.

This really is a shot that requires practice, and you also need a fairly good lie to play it. Do not attempt it if the ball is sitting down, or if you are on really closely cut grass.

Make a positive high follow through.

Make a positive swing.

Accelerate through the ball on impact.

LOB SHOT TIPS

- Open the clubface.

- Position the ball forward of centre.

- Slide the club under the ball on impact.

PLAYING
THE GAME

PLAYING THE GAME

So far in this book you have learned the basic techniques for the majority of shots that you will face on the course. The following section deals with some of the key situations in which you will find yourself when playing a round of golf. What happens when you don't get the perfect lie, or if you are on a slope? How do you play a shot when you land in the rough and you get a bad lie? You need to be able to recover from these situations, and you will learn how to do so as you read the following pages.

Most rounds will involve unorthodox shots at some time or another.

Think through your strategy, even on short holes.

During the course of this chapter you will learn what to do in all these situations and more. You will be taught how to play from an upslope, downslope, and both side slopes. The most important thing to remember when playing from a sloping lie is not to fight the slope, but to make a few small set up changes, and use the slope to your advantage.

You will also learn how to play shots from the rough. Again, this need not be too difficult, but you need to know how the ball will react from various lies with both full shots, and from shorter shots closer to the green.

Sometimes when you are playing you will need to deliberately hit the ball left-to-right or right-to-left. These shots will be covered, as will deliberately hitting the ball higher and lower than normal. All these different shots are required to reach a good level skill at the game, so learn and practise them as often as possible.

Course strategy is also very important, and in the following pages you will see examples of a game plan for tackling various holes. It will also cover the questions of when should you attack and when you should defend.

Don't be too "greedy" when playing out of traps – just get the ball on the fairway.

BALL ABOVE YOUR FEET

During a round of golf, unless you play on a completely flat course (and there are very few of those around!), you will be faced with shots when the ball is on a sloping lie and is higher or lower than your feet. Here we're going to look at how to play the ball when it is above your feet. The tendency with this shot is for you to either hit the ground behind the ball, or, if you do make good contact for the ball, to go left (or if you're left-handed to shoot off to the right).

Following the GASPS routine outlined here, you will be able to play the ball cleanly and accurately.

GRIP
When playing the ball above your feet, your swing will naturally flatten out. To counter this it is essential to grip down the club. How far you should "choke down" depends on the severity of the slope. Take your normal grip, and if you are on a gentle slope you should grip down by about an inch, but if the slope is steep you may find that you'll need to hold the club right down at the bottom of the grip.

AIM AND ALIGNMENT
As described earlier, your swing will naturally be flatter when the ball is above your feet, and this will cause the ball to draw or hook to the left (or right for left-handers). Because of this you need to aim the club and align your body to the right (or left). Again, it is difficult to say how far off you should aim because it will change with the severity of the slope. With practice and experience you'll quickly begin to judge how far off to aim.

Grip down the club.

Your weight will naturally fall onto your heels.

Aim off to the right.

STANCE AND BALL POSITION

Your stance should remain as it would for a normal swing, but it is really important to move the ball back in your stance. This again is needed to combat the flatter swing that you will use for this shot. If you don't move the ball back in your stance you are likely to hit the ground behind the ball. Once again, you need to experiment with how far back to move the ball, depending on the severity of the slope.

POSTURE

Your weight will naturally have been pushed back toward your heels because you are standing on a slope. Do not fight this. You will also find that you will naturally be standing more upright than you normally would. Again, this is something you should just allow to happen – it is this that creates the flatter swing, and you will have compensated for this with your grip and the realignment of your aim.

SWING

The swing will naturally be flatter and the arc of the club will be more around your body. To recreate and become used to this sensation, make some practice swings. As you do, pretend that you are trying to hit a ball off a tee that is 12in (30cm) high. Do this and you will feel your swing naturally flatten out. This is how your swing should feel when the ball is above your feet.

Learn the key set up changes needed to play this shot, and don't forget the ball is likely to curve to the left. Do not fight it, just trust your swing.

Your swing will naturally flatten out.

BALL BELOW YOUR FEET

The tendency for shots when the ball is lying below your feet is to either hit the ball thin (that is, halfway up the ball rather than crisply underneath), or, if you do strike it well, for the ball to slice to the right. It is a really difficult shot to play, because it is hard to retain your balance. As you swing, if you try and fight the slope you will lose your balance forward and will find that you have too much weight falling toward your toes. This can have disastrous results.

Follow the GASPS instructions below, then practise this shot. It doesn't have to be destructive, but you must make the correct adjustments.

GRIP
Whenever the ball is below your feet it is essential to grip the club right at the top of the grip, with the effect of lengthening the club – to help you cope with the slope.

AIM AND ALIGNMENT
Because the ball is below your feet, which will automatically make you swing more upright than normal, the ball will invariably curve from left-to-right (or the other way if you're left-handed) in the air. Do not try to fight this, just aim to the left (or right) of the target with your body and the club and let the ball curve back toward it.

STANCE AND BALL POSITION
Your stance should be the same as for a normal shot, but the ball should be moved more toward your front foot.

POSTURE
This is the most critical element with this shot. A lot of people try and fight the slope and put their weight back

Hold the very top of the grip.

Play the ball more off the front foot.

Your swing will naturally be more upright.

into their heels. However, this is completely wrong because as you swing, your weight will be pulled forward down the slope, which will have the effect of moving you closer to the ball. This can also lead to a shank, which is when you strike the ball with the base of the shaft (the hosel) rather than the clubface. Remember, do not fight the slope. Set yourself up so that your weight goes with the slope, and will therefore be on your toes at set up. This will mean that your posture is slightly more bent over than normal – compensate for this by bending the knees a little more than normal.

SWING

Balance is the key to making this swing correctly. Try and stay as grounded as possible, and use a little less leg action than you would normally. As mentioned, your swing will naturally be a little more upright – don't fight against this, just trust yourself and remember that the ball will curve from left-to-right (or right-to-left).

Without doubt this is one of the hardest shots in golf, but if you make the set up changes described above you will give yourself a good chance of making a successful shot. Like all aspects of golf, it will require a lot of practice, but once you have spent some time on it then it need not fill you with fear. Trust your swing.

BALL BELOW YOUR FEET TIPS

- Grip the very top of the club.

- Aim the ball slightly to the left of your target.

- Flex your knees more than normal.

Bend your knees more at the set up.

Stay as grounded as possible during the shot.

BALL ON AN UPSLOPE

Playing a shot from an upslope is comparatively easy. It is simple to make a good strike, and if you remember that the ball will go higher than normal, and will tend to fly right-to-left (or left-to-right if you're left-handed) in the air, you should soon be able to master this shot. Because you'll be swinging up the slope, the ball will fly higher than normal, and therefore not travel as far. To compensate, take an extra club – where you would hit a 6-iron from ball to green, you should "club up" and hit a 5-iron.

Follow the GASPS instructions outlined here and you'll find playing a ball on an upslope a relatively straightforward shot.

GRIP
Take your normal grip, but make sure you grip the club at its full length to avoid hitting the ball thin.

AIM AND ALIGNMENT
The tendency with this shot is for the ball to draw from right-to-left (or left-to-right), therefore it is important for you to aim to the right (or left) and to just allow for the curve in your shot.

STANCE AND BALL POSITION
Because you are on an upslope, it is difficult to get your legs to work properly in your swing. Therefore it is a good idea to narrow your stance. This will give you more freedom in the legs, and encourage them to work correctly in the swing. Try to set your body weight with the slope, not against it – so for this shot you need to set more weight on your back foot. How much will depend on the severity of the slope. Move the ball position forward in your stance, toward your front foot.

Grip the club at its full length.

Play the ball more off the front foot.

Allow more flex in your front knee.

POSTURE

You should have a little more flex in your front knee than your back one. This is because you have more weight on the back foot, and it will also help you to align your hips and shoulders so that they are parallel to the slope. Doing this will enable you to make good contact with the ball.

SWING

Try to encourage the sensation of swinging the club up the slope. It is hard to get your weight moving correctly with this shot, so it is important that when you swing back and your weight goes into your back foot, you need to try and stay steady and centred. Do not sway backward. As you make your downswing into impact, really make an extra effort to get your weight through and forward. As you do this, try to swing the club up the slope. If the slope is very severe, do not worry if you lose a little balance back down the slope, but you must make sure it happens after the ball has left the club.

Remember not to fight the slope. Set yourself up so that your body is parallel to it. Make sure you swing up the slope, and try to get the legs working as well as you can. Practise this shot and you will find yourself able to launch the ball well.

UPSLOPE TIPS

- Aim off to the right (or left for left-handers).

- Narrow your stance.

- Get your weight through and forward.

Set more weight on the back foot.

Avoid swaying backward.

BALL ON A DOWNSLOPE

This shot is much harder than playing from an upslope, but once again if you make the correct set up adjustments you'll quickly master it. Because you are playing the ball from a downslope, the club will be de-lofted at impact. This means that the ball will fly lower and travel further than it would from a flat lie – exactly opposite to playing the ball on an upslope. To allow for this you need to go down a club – if the shot would normally be a 7-iron distance, you should change to an 8-iron.

Here are the GASPS instructions for a downsloping lie.

GRIP
Hold the club as normal, but grip down slightly. The tendency when playing from a downslope is to hit the ground behind the ball. Choking down on the grip will help to stop this from happening.

AIM AND ALIGNMENT
The ball will normally curve from left-to-right (or right-to-left for left-handers) when playing from a downslope, therefore it is important to align your body to the left

(or right) of the target, and make sure your clubface is also aimed to the left (or right).

STANCE AND BALL POSITION
Because you are on a downslope, your legs will tend to be overactive in your swing. To compensate for this you should widen your stance. Widening your stance stops your legs from working too much when you swing. It is vital to set your body with the slope, so you should put more weight than normal on your front foot. The tendency is to hit this shot heavy or fat (that is, behind the ball) so you need to move the ball back in your stance, toward

Grip down the club to avoid hitting the ground behind the ball.

Widen your stance to keep leg movement to a minimum.

Aim to the left (or right for left-handers) of the target.

Don't try to "lift" the ball into the air – trust the club.

your back foot. This will help you to catch the ball first instead of the ground.

POSTURE

With more weight than normal on your front foot, you will also need to flex the back knee a little more. This will help you to align your hips and shoulders parallel to the slope.

SWING

When the ball is on a downslope it is very tempting to try to deliberately lift it into the air. You must avoid this, and instead try to swing with the slope and feel like you're "chasing" the ball down the slope. The changes that you have made to your set up will have encouraged a slightly steeper than normal swing, which is vital. Trust these changes, and remember not to try and lift the ball – let the loft of the club do that for you.

The ball will fly lower, and will curve from left-to-right (or right-to-left) in the air. Don't fight this, just accept the fact that it is going to happen, and make the correct set up adjustments. This shot is quite difficult, so make sure that you practise it.

DOWNSLOPE TIPS

- Hold the grip slightly down the club.

- Flex your back knee.

- Feel as if you're "chasing" the ball down the slope.

Play the ball further back toward the back foot.

Flex the back knee more than the front.

Try to get the feeling of "chasing" the ball down the slope as you swing through the shot.

THE DELIBERATE DRAW

There will be occasions on the course when you need to deliberately draw the ball – curve it from right-to-left (or left-to-right for left-handers). You might have a tree in your way and need to get round it, or you may be on the tee of a hole that "doglegs" from right-to-left and you want to curve the ball around it (left-handed players need to fade the ball – see pages 118–19). This also allows a more experienced player, who is playing a shot with a strong left-to-right wind, to learn to hold the ball straight into the wind.

The draw is also a more powerful shot that will generate more distance. Let's take a look at the GASPS routine.

GRIP
Slightly close the clubface and then take your grip. This will give you a "strong" grip that will help to encourage the draw. How much to close the face depends on how much you want the ball to curve in the air – the more you close it, the more it will draw.

AIM AND ALIGNMENT
Align your feet, knees, hips, and shoulders on a line with where you want the ball to start, and the clubface to a point where you want the ball to finish.

STANCE AND BALL POSITION
Your stance should be as normal, but move the ball back in your stance a little bit, so that you're playing the shot with the ball in the middle of your feet rather than slightly forward, as you normally would when playing a mid- to long iron.

Slightly close the clubface.

Feel the bottom wrist rolling over the top.

POSTURE

There is no need to change from your normal posture when drawing the ball.

SWING

With your feet aligned to the right (or left for left-handers), and your clubface pointing at the target, the idea is to make your normal swing along the line of your feet. This should make the ball start on the line of your feet and then, due to the fact that the clubface is closed, curve to the left (or right) in the air.

If you are struggling to get the ball to curve, you need to practise a feeling of really releasing the club through impact, or trying to feel that you are rolling the bottom hand and wrist over the top. To encourage this, practise gripping the club a little softer than normal. Imagine hitting a forehand topspin drive down the line in tennis. Visualise the way you need to roll your wrist over the racket as you make contact with the ball. Hitting a draw requires a very similar feeling.

Remember that this shot is very powerful, so when hitting an iron shot to a green, you may need to take one less club than you would normally need for that distance.

DRAW TIPS

- Close the clubface slightly before taking your grip.

- Move the ball back in your stance.

- Try to feel your wrists rolling over on impact.

Swing along the line parallel to your feet.

For right-handers, the ball will curve from right to left.

THE DELIBERATE FADE

As with the deliberate draw, covered on pages 116–117, there will also be occasions during a round when you will need to curve the ball from left-to-right in the air. You may have to get round an obstacle, or you may wish to shape a tee shot to fit a left-to-right dogleg hole. Again, the more experienced player may wish to hit a fade into a right-to-left wind to help keep the ball straight. And naturally, where a right-handed player needs to fade the ball, a left-handed player will need to draw it and vice versa.

Here are the GASPS to help you hit the deliberate fade.

GRIP
Slightly open the clubface, and then take your grip as normal. How much you open the clubface depends on how much you want the ball to curve in the air.

AIM AND ALIGNMENT
Aim your body to the left (or right) of the target, on a line with where you want the ball to start. Now aim the clubface at the target.

STANCE AND BALL POSITION
Your stance should remain the same as it would be for a normal shot of the same distance, but you should move the ball forward in your stance and position it closer to the front foot than normal.

POSTURE
There is no change needed from your normal posture.

SWING
The idea of this shot is to swing the club along the line of your feet. Because the clubface is open to that line, the ball should start left of the target and then curve back

Feel as if you're slicing under and across the ball.

toward it. If you can't get the ball to curve, you need to try to get the feeling of delaying the release of the club, so try to keep the club open through impact. To help you to achieve this, grip the club a little tighter than normal in the top hand. This has the effect of shortening the muscles in your arm, and stops them from releasing the club at impact.

To get a visual image of the swing required to hit this shot, imagine a tennis player hitting a forehand slice. Picture how they would need to swing the racket across their body and hold the racket face open as they hit the shot.

Try this shot on the driving range. Remember, it is a weaker shot than normal and you may need to hit an extra club. You can sometimes use this to your advantage when you are playing. If you have 150yds (135m) to the flag, and you hit a normal 7-iron 145yds (130m) and a normal 6-iron 160yds (145m), it can be difficult to find a shot to go the correct distance. Why not hit a 6-iron with a little fade?

With the fade going slightly shorter than a normal shot, it would be perfect to use in this example.

FADE TIPS

- Slightly open the clubface.

- Move the ball forward in your stance.

- Grip slightly tighter than normal with the top hand.

Again, swing along the line parallel to your feet.

For right-handers, the ball will fade from left to right.

HIT THE BALL HIGHER

On the course there will be times when you want to add loft to a particular shot, by hitting it higher than normal. You may have to hit over a tree, or you may be playing with the wind behind you and want to add distance to the shot by hitting it high and letting it ride the wind. You can also use this shot if the flag is cut just over a bunker, and you want to hit the ball higher and therefore stop it quicker on the green. The key to playing this shot lies with the set up. A few simple adjustments can really alter the flight of the ball.

Let's take a look at the GASPS tips for this shot.

GRIP
No changes are needed, so set up with your normal grip.

AIM AND ALIGNMENT
No changes are required from your normal position.

STANCE AND BALL POSITION
Open your stance a little wider than normal, and move the ball forward toward your front foot. By moving the ball forward you are effectively adding approximately three degrees of loft to the club, which is vital when trying to launch the ball higher.

Your stance should be wider than normal.

Play the ball more off the front foot.

Head stays behind the ball at impact.

POSTURE

Stand a little bit closer to the ball. By standing closer you are forcing yourself into a slightly more upright posture. This will lead to a more upright swing, which will help you to get the ball in the air.

SWING

Let your set up changes dictate the swing. As you swing the club through impact, try and feel that your head stays behind the ball. Finish the swing with your hands nice and high over your front shoulder. While it is important to not try to lift this shot by swinging up at the ball, you definitely need to feel that you are helping it up by swinging up with your follow through.

Swing hard into impact. A ball that flies high will normally fly a little bit shorter, so you need to be really positive at impact. The other benefit of hitting the shot hard is that it adds backspin to the shot. Backspin will make the ball rise up higher than normal.

It's important to remember not to deliberately try to "lift" the ball higher into the air. Follow the instructions here and trust to your swing – after a bit of practice, hitting higher will become second nature.

HITTING HIGHER TIPS

- Move the ball forward in your stance.
- Swing hard at impact.
- Finish the swing with high follow through.

Stand slightly closer to the ball.

Swing harder into the impact.

Finish with hands high over the front shoulder.

HIT THE BALL LOWER

This is another vital shot in the repertoire of all good golfers. The ability to hit the ball very low can rescue you from many difficult positions. If you are in the trees and need to get the ball back into play, hitting it low is usually the best option. It is also a useful shot to play on windy days. Keeping the ball down and out of the wind is vital to scoring well when playing in windy conditions. Tiger Woods is a master of this shot – you'll often see him hitting "the stinger" where the ball "drills" away very low.

To emulate Tiger, follow the GASPS tips outlined here.

GRIP
Take your normal grip and then choke down the club a little bit. The further down the grip you go, the easier it is to hit the ball lower.

AIM AND ALIGNMENT
This shot will normally have a little right-to-left (or left-to-right for left-handers) curve on the ball, so it is a good idea to aim a little to the right (left) of your intended target.

STANCE AND BALL POSITION
Narrow your stance a little bit, and move the ball toward your back foot. The further back you move it, the lower it will fly. Keep your hands forward toward your front thigh, so that your hands are well ahead of the ball. Your weight should favour your front side with approximately 60% of your body weight on your front foot. This position of having the ball back in your stance, and the weight forward, is essential for success with this shot.

Hold the club slightly lower down the grip.

"Punch" through the ball on impact.

POSTURE

With your weight forward, your body will also naturally be leaning forward slightly. No other changes in your posture are needed to play this shot.

SWING

Try to keep the club low to the ground on the backswing – you are trying to shallow out your swing to promote a low ball flight. Do not allow your weight to move too far back during your backswing. As you swing into impact, make sure your hands are leading the clubhead into the ball. Try to feel that your head and body are over the ball when you strike it. If your head is behind the ball at impact, it will go too high. Match your follow through to the ball flight that you want by keeping it nice and low, and not swinging through to your normal finish. Get the sensation of "punching" the ball forward.

HITTING LOWER TIPS

- Move the ball back in your stance.

- Keep your hands ahead of the ball.

- "Punch" the ball to the target.

Play the ball off the back foot.

Ensure your hands lead at impact.

Keep a low follow through for a low flight.

THE FAIRWAY BUNKER SHOT

This shot is completely different from the greenside bunker shots covered earlier – here, you're looking for good distance. The first thing to do is assess the lie of the ball, as well as how steep the lip is on the front of the bunker. If you have a good lie and not much lip to go over, you can hit just about any iron you want from the trap. If there is a lip, remember your first priority is to get the ball out of the bunker, so you must choose a club with enough loft to comfortably clear the lip in front of you.

If you're not confident hitting long irons, try using a hybrid or rescue club or even a lofted wood – there's nothing in the rules that says you can't use a wood out of a sand trap. Once you have decided what club to hit, follow the GASPS sequence below to help with the technique required to play the shot well.

GRIP
Take your normal grip, and then choke down the grip by about 1in (2.5cm). A great grip tip for long bunker shots is to feel that you are stretching your thumbs down the grip. This has the effect of restricting your wrist action during your swing, and that will really help you play this shot well.

Choke down the grip, and feel your thumbs "stretching" down.

Aim off slightly to the left (or right for left-handers).

Take the ball cleanly off the top of the sand.

You'll notice a slightly shallower swing plane.

AIM AND ALIGNMENT

Due to restricting your wrist action for this shot, the ball will tend to have a slight left-to-right shape, or right-to-left for left-handers. To compensate for this, you should aim your body and your club slightly to the left (or right).

STANCE AND BALL POSITION

Slightly widen your stance to help keep your leg action to a minimum, and shuffle your feet into the sand to give a firm base from which to swing. Move the ball back to the centre of your stance.

POSTURE

The only change to your standard posture is that you should stand slightly taller than normal, making for a more upright swing that will encourage you to contact the ball before the sand. Failure to contact the ball before the sand leads to a heavy shot that will not have sufficient distance.

SWING

Try to clip the ball cleanly off the top of the sand. Stretching your thumbs down the grip, as described earlier, will help you to do this, due to the restricted wrist action. Try and swing wider than normal, which will give you a shallower swing plane. This will help you to get the correct contact. If you find that you are hitting the sand behind the ball

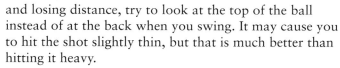

FAIRWAY BUNKER TIPS

- Feel as if you're stretching your thumbs down the grip.

- Widen your stance.

- Clip the ball cleanly off the top of the sand.

and losing distance, try to look at the top of the ball instead of at the back when you swing. It may cause you to hit the shot slightly thin, but that is much better than hitting it heavy.

Because you are gripping down the club slightly, you may need to hit with one more club than you normally would. So, if you would normally hit with a 6-iron, try with a 5-iron. Practise hitting shots from a fairway sand trap, and not only will your bunker play improve, you will also improve your ball striking for normal iron shots.

Play the ball in the centre of your feet.

Swing wider than you would normally.

Accelerate through the ball at impact.

Finish with hands high above your front shoulder.

PLAYING FROM THE ROUGH

Playing shots from the light rough should pose few problems. Make your normal swing and allow for the fact that the ball will roll a little further when it lands due to the lack of backspin. However, when you're in thicker rough you need to make a few adjustments to play the shot well. You need to assess the lie and decide what club to hit. The worse the lie the more lofted the club you should use – and if your ball is sitting down in really thick rough, the best strategy is just to wedge it back out onto the fairway.

Remember, if you hit it in the rough in the first place, and if you wedge it back into play and it costs you a shot, it is not the end of the world. If you are too greedy and try to gain too much distance from a really bad lie it can end up costing you two or even more shots. Don't fall into this trap.

In order to hit a shot from a bad lie, try the following GASPS changes.

GRIP
Hold the club tighter than normal. There is a tendency for the thick grass to wrap around the neck of the club, which has the effect of closing the clubface and making you hit way to the left (or right for left-handers). By gripping tighter you are going some way to eliminating this.

A typical shot from the rough, with just the top half of the ball visible.

Grip the club slightly tighter than you would normally, to stop it twisting in your hands.

Stand with your feet slightly wider apart to help ground yourself.

AIM AND ALIGNMENT

When you have a really bad lie, aim a little to the right (or left) to compensate for the clubface closing at impact when it tangles with the long grass.

STANCE

Stand a little wider than normal. You are going to hit this shot hard, so a good firm base is vital for this shot. Move the ball back in the stance, and set up with a little more weight than normal on the front side, with about 60% of your body weight on your front foot. How far back in the stance to move the ball depends on how bad the lie is, but try playing it just behind centre for most shots.

POSTURE

Adopt a slight forward lean because your weight is favouring your front foot. Apart from this, try to keep your posture the same.

SWING

Make a really steep, powerful swing to explode the ball out of the rough. With your weight set on your front side it will make you swing up slightly steeper than normal, which will allow you to hit down hard onto the back of the ball. Remember to keep your grip pressure tight. You should

PLAYING FROM THE ROUGH TIPS

- Hold the club tighter than you normally would.

- Aim a little to the right of the target if you have a really bad lie.

- Swing down steeply and hard on the back of the ball.

remove a sizeable chunk of turf with this shot, which will probably restrict your follow through. Don't worry, as long as you have made a powerful hit into the back of the ball, it should come out.

Practise from various different lies to see which clubs you can hit from which lies. Sometimes a lofted wood or hybrid (rescue) club can work quite well from an intermediate lie. Give it a try!

Make a powerful steep downswing but without hitting from the top.

Explode the ball out of the rough, taking a good divot with it.

Don't worry if your follow through feels more restricted than normal.

PAR 3 STRATEGY

Strategy and course management play an absolutely vital part in learning to play the game, and getting the best score possible every time you're out on the course. Par 3 holes, while they are the shortest, are often the most difficult on which to make par (achieve the standard score for a hole). They can vary in length from 100yds (90m) up to 250yds (230m). The shorter ones tend to have very small and tricky greens, whereas the longer ones obviously require a really well-struck tee shot to give you the best chance of scoring well.

How to approach Par 3 holes really does depend on your ability. Here are two examples of different Par 3 holes, with a suggested way of playing them for the low handicapper (nine or less), the intermediate handicapper (10–18), and the improving player (handicap 18 and above).

The first aim for the low handicapper is to make par on these holes – that is, to complete each hole in three strokes. If you can par all the Par 3s in a round it puts you well on the way to shooting a good round. If you happen to make a birdie (score one under par on an individual hole), treat it as a bonus – focus on trying to make par.

The intermediate handicapper needs to assess the difficulty of the hole. On the shorter Par 3s you should be aiming to make par; on the longer Par 3s you should still be aiming for a par, but make sure that you make no more than four. For example, if there is water all the way down the right side, and lots of space to the left of the green, aim to the left of the green and avoid the water. This way, the worst you will make is four and you will have (hopefully) avoided making double bogey (scoring two under par) or worse.

The improving player should approach Par 3 holes slightly differently. You get a shot on all of them, so making a four actually gives you a net three with your handicap allowance. Bear this in mind when deciding how to play the hole. Play safe and do not be too aggressive. Your aim is to make a four at all the Par 3s. If you happen to make the odd three then great – treat it as a bonus and go to the next tee happy. Try and avoid the disaster of making five or even more. Keeping serious mistakes to a minimum is the best way for you to improve your scores.

Remember, Par 3 holes, although short, should be treated with respect. Think about your strategy, make a decision on the tee, and then trust it as you play the hole.

Even simple-looking Par 3s can be fraught with tricky situations.

PAR 3 TIPS

● Assess the hole based on your ability.

● Don't take unnecessary risks.

● Stick with your strategy.

Length of hole
240yds (219m)

Length of hole 210yds
(192m)

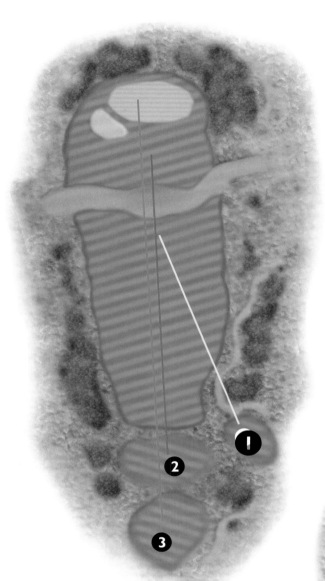

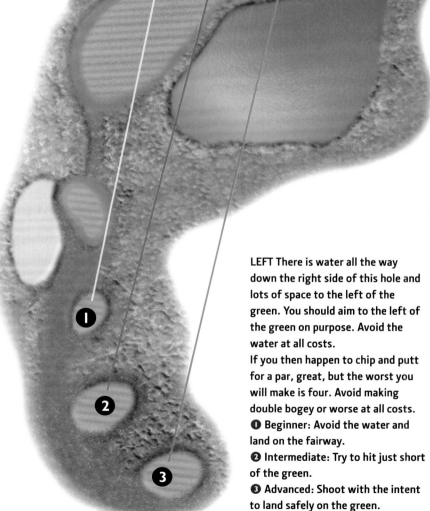

ABOVE There is a hazard in the form of a stream running across the fairway, about three-quarters of the way down the length of the hole. This must be avoided or else severe penalties will result. Short hitters should lay up in front of the hazard and play a second shot over and onto the green, hopefully making a four or even a three.

❶ Beginner: Play safe and hit a comfortable mid-iron just short of the hazard.

❷ Intermediate: You should have the distance to go for the green, but don't worry if you're short.

❸ Advanced: Aim for the green.

LEFT There is water all the way down the right side of this hole and lots of space to the left of the green. You should aim to the left of the green on purpose. Avoid the water at all costs.

If you then happen to chip and putt for a par, great, but the worst you will make is four. Avoid making double bogey or worse at all costs.

❶ Beginner: Avoid the water and land on the fairway.

❷ Intermediate: Try to hit just short of the green.

❸ Advanced: Shoot with the intent to land safely on the green.

PAR 4 STRATEGY

Par 4 holes are the most common of all the holes on a standard 18-hole golf course – with most courses having at least ten examples. Naturally, with so many Par 4s on any given course, they vary dramatically in difficulty and the tactics required differ depending on the length of the hole and how narrow it is. A Par 4 can be as short as 270yds (250m), but as long as 500yds (450m). Once again, you need to realistically assess your ability on the tee before making a decision on how to play the hole.

Opposite are two examples of different Par 4 holes, with a suggested way of playing them for the low handicapper (nine or less), the intermediate handicapper (10–18), and the improving player (handicap 18 and above).

The first aim for the low handicapper is to get the ball on the fairway off the tee. On the shorter Par 4s, which are often tighter with more trouble than other holes, it can be prudent to hit a fairway wood, or even a long iron off the tee to make sure you get the ball in play. Do not automatically reach for the driver on the tee. Plot your strategy well, and then stick with it. However, there could be a short Par 4 that you can reach from the tee with a good drive. Again, you need to see what trouble is around before you decide if it is worth the gamble. There is nothing more satisfying than driving a Par 4 and having an eagle putt (two under par), but there is nothing worse than trying to drive a short Par 4, hitting it in trouble and making double bogey (two over par) or worse. Discretion often is the best part of valour! Make a decision and stick with it.

The intermediate handicapper will need to assess the difficulty of the hole while standing on the tee. Try to get the ball on the fairway at all costs, even if it means hitting a 3-wood from the tee and sacrificing some distance. At the short Par 4s don't go for heroics, find the fairway, find the green, and make a par. On the longer Par 4s, don't worry if you make five, but avoid running up a big score by being too ambitious.

The improving player should approach Par 4s slightly differently. Imagine that, for you, they are a Par 5. Try to plan an easy way to get the ball on the green in three shots. This could mean leaving the driver in the bag and playing a sensible tee shot with an iron or fairway wood. Remember, plan the hole and try to stick with the plan. Avoid making six or worse at all costs. If you do find yourself in trouble at any point, do not go for a miraculous escape shot, just get the ball back in play and move on.

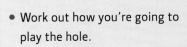
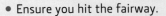

PAR 4 TIPS

- Work out how you're going to play the hole.

- Ensure you hit the fairway.

- Don't be too ambitious in what you attempt.

Looking back down an inviting Par 4 fairway.

BELOW This dogleg Par 4 has a sand trap and a stream further up the fairway.
❶ Beginner: Aim to get the ball on the fairway. Fly the stream with the second shot, and land on the green with the third.
❷ Intermediate: Lay up before the stream, then try to run up and onto the green with the second shot.
❸ Advanced: Clearing the stream with a good drive should leave a short approach.

RIGHT A shortish straight Par 4 should offer scoring opportunities for the advanced and maybe intermediate player.
❶ Beginner: Avoid the bunker, and aim to get to the green in three shots.
❷ Intermediate: Try to clear the bunker, leaving a short iron to the green.
❸ Advanced: If you're hitting well, reaching the green in one might be feasible; otherwise, you'll be left only with a lob.

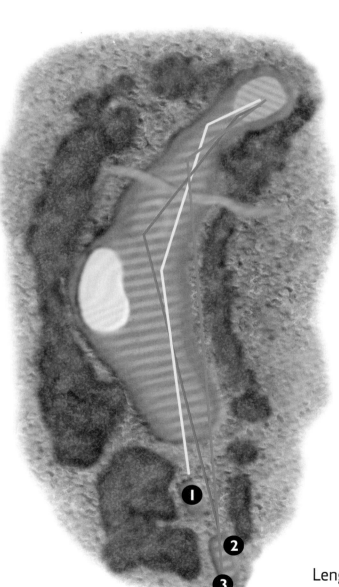

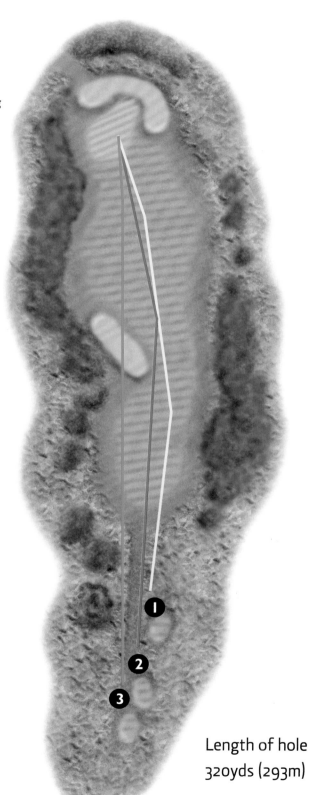

Length of hole
380yds (347m)

Length of hole
320yds (293m)

PAR 5 STRATEGY

Par 5 holes are the longest holes on any golf course and can be anything from 471yds (450m) to 690yds (630 m). For the improving player, they are probably the most difficult, purely because of their length, which requires the player to hit at least two or three long clubs. But for the low handicapper, they are often the easiest and usually offer the best chance of a birdie. As the holes are longer, you should definitely have a clear game plan before embarking on any Par 5 hole.

Opposite are two examples of different Par 5 holes, with a suggested way of playing them for the low handicapper (nine or less), the intermediate handicapper (10–18), and the improving player (handicap 18 and above).

For the low handicapper, you should really be thinking of a Par 5 as a birdie opportunity. Can you reach the green in two? If you can, and there is not too much trouble around, then give it a go. If you can't reach the green in two, ask yourself where you would like to be playing your third shot from then plot the easiest way of hitting your first two shots to that point. Playing the hole backward in your mind is a great way of coming up with a good strategy. Because Par 5s are the easiest holes for

the good golfer, they are often designed with awkward greens that are well-protected by bunkers or other hazards. Sometimes leaving yourself a full shot in for your third shot (so that you can get some backspin and control the ball) is easier than leaving yourself a 40-yd (36-m) half shot that is difficult to judge. Take all these things into account before tackling the hole.

The intermediate handicapper should look on a Par 5 as a good opportunity of making a par. You can normally comfortably reach the green in three shots, which will leave you two putts for par. Once again plot the easiest way of making sure you stay out of trouble, and if it means not hitting the driver, then don't hit it. Sometimes the best way to play a tight or narrow Par 5 can be to hit a 5-iron off the tee, 5-iron second shot and a 5-iron to the green. This may sound defensive, but can be very successful.

For the improving player, Par 5s can be quite intimidating. If you don't hit the ball that far they can seem like very long holes that never end. Do not fall into the trap of trying to hit the ball too hard to gain extra distance. Make sure that you get the ball in play off the tee. If you hit a nice straight tee shot, even if not all that long, it then means you have a good lie in order to get good distance on your next shot. Going for a big drive, hitting it in trouble, and then having to chip out sideways can be very costly. Four nice steady shots should see you somewhere near the green, which gives you the opportunity of making a five or six.

There's water and trees to contend with around this green.

BELOW A relatively straight-forward Par 5 should be viewed as a scoring chance for all advanced and many intermediates.
❶ Beginner: Just keep the ball on the fairway and hit three or even four gentle shots to the green.
❷ Intermediate: Again, priority for the fairway but a short pitch for the third shot should be on.
❸ Advanced: You might reach in two, but certainly a very short third, leaving you pin high.

RIGHT With water around, beginners and intermediates should play safe and approach the green from the right.
❶ Beginner: Again, hit the fairway, avoid the water on the left and hit the green in three.
❷ Intermediate: Aim right of the water and right of the green with the second – you may get up.
❸ Advanced: Lay up short of the water, but fly to the green with a good second shot.

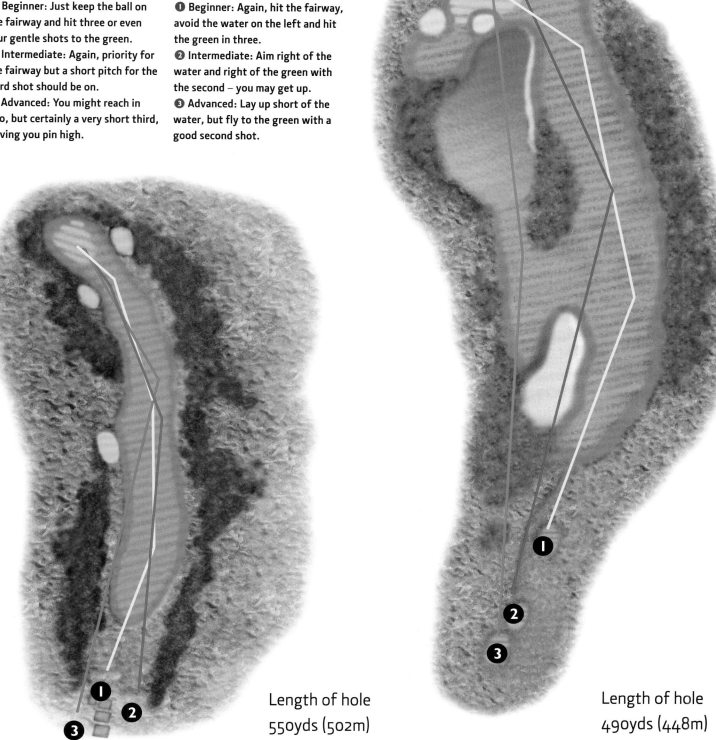

Length of hole
550yds (502m)

Length of hole
490yds (448m)

FAULTS AND FIXES

FAULTS AND FIXES

No matter how well you have learned to play, or how good a player you become, there will always be occasions when things aren't going as well as you would like with your game. This is the nature of the game of golf. It affects all players, from the relative newcomer to the seasoned professional. Golf can be the most frustrating game in the world, but all those hours of despair and frustration seem to vanish when a new tip or lesson works and you suddenly start hitting the ball well again.

The leading players in the world all employ the services of coaches and professionals to keep an eye on their set up and swing, and you should do the same. A qualified professional is trained to see your faults and to help you fix them in the shortest possible time. A lesson, or series of lessons, is the best investment you will ever make in your golfing career.

FINDING A CURE

Many people pay a lot of money for new clubs or balls in the hope that they will magically transform their game. Don't do this if you are not prepared to pay for a few lessons – lessons will be much better value and give you much better results.

All golfers, no matter what standard, will find faults creeping in.

The practice ground, not the course, is the place to work on your swing.

There is often a simple reason that things have gone awry in your swing. Many times the problems you are having will stem back to a fault in your set up.

Over the next few pages you will be shown some of the most common bad shots that can creep into your game, together with a checklist of the things that may be causing it.

TECHNIQUES TO FIX YOUR GAME

The checklist will appear in the GASPS formula. Go through it in the correct order and, with a lot of practice and a little bit of trial and error, you will help yourself get out of the bad habits.

As you work through the exercises, you will see that a lot of bad shots are closely related. The slice and the pull are basically caused by the same swing problem, and the hook and the push are caused by another. Even if you are not experiencing the particular problems that are described, it is worth reading them all because it will help you to obtain a good knowledge of the swing, and what can go wrong with it. If you understand what can go wrong, it will help you to avoid these common pitfalls in the future and give you a clearer understanding of what you should be doing to achieve a good swing.

FIXING TIPS

- Go back to basics and begin with the set up.

- One or two lessons will provide a better return than a new driver.

- Work through the exercises shown in this section.

A few lessons with the pro will put you back on track.

THE SLICE

The slice is possibly the most regular bad shot in the game. The ball starts to the left (or right for left-handers) of the target, and then curves dramatically to the right (or left). It is very difficult to hit the fairway from the tee if you slice, and you will tend to only ever see the right (or left) side of the course! The slice is also a weak shot, and a lot of distance is lost if you slice the ball. A slice is caused by swinging the club from out-to-in across the ball-to-target line, with the clubface to the right (or left) of that swing path at impact.

Let's have a look at the GASPS formula that will help you overcome a slice.

GRIP

Check that your grip is not in a weak position. Remember that your top thumb should be just right (or left for left-handers) of centre and you should be able to see two or three knuckles on the back of your top hand. If your grip is too far to the left (or right) you will only see one knuckle, or even no knuckle at all. Your bottom-hand grip should be in the fingers, with the palm of your hand facing the target. Don't let your bottom hand get too much on top of the club.

AIM AND ALIGNMENT

Check that your clubface is not aiming to the right (or left) of your intended target at address. With your alignment, it is vital to keep your feet, knees, hips and shoulders parallel to your target line. When you slice, it is tempting to align yourself too far to the left (or right) to compensate for the ball flight, however, this will force you to swing across the ball-to-target line and slice the ball even more.

STANCE AND BALL POSITION

Your stance may be too narrow, in which case your upper body will become overactive in the swing. Remember your

FAULTS

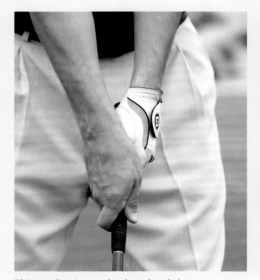

This weak grip may lead to sliced shots.

An open clubface will send the ball off course.

Check the alignment of your feet.

feet should be shoulder width apart, and even wider with a wood. Additionally, the ball may be positioned too far forward in your stance, which will force you to lean forward to reach the ball and therefore open your shoulders too much.

POSTURE

Make sure you are not too bent over at address, and that you do not have too much weight on your toes. These faults can cause you to swing too upright, which creates a slice swing.

SWING

If you are confident that your set up is correct and you are still slicing, then there must be a problem with your swing. There could be many reasons for this, but you should deal with the open clubface first. When you slice the ball, your clubface must be open to the line of your swing. To help get out of this fault, first try to grip the club a little softer, which will help your hands work better in the swing. Second, try to rotate your forearms at impact. Exaggerate the feeling and imagine that you are trying to get the bottom wrist to roll over the top of the top wrist at impact. Don't worry if you hit a few shots to the left (or right) to start with – if this happens, just roll the wrists slightly less until you get it right.

Feeling your wrists turn over will often cure a slice.

The ball is too far forward.

Swinging outside the line.

Swing is too upright.

THE PULL

The pull shot is when the ball starts to the left (or to the right for left-handers) of the target, and carries on going left (or right) as it flies. The shot has many similarities to a slice in that it is caused by swinging across the line of the ball. The big difference is that with the pull, the clubface is square or closed to the out-to-in swing path, rather than open, as it is with the slice. There are a number of reasons why golfers pull the ball, but all are pretty easy to cure.

If you've had a nasty experience with a pull shot recently, have a look at the GASPS changes and they'll more than likely help you out.

GRIP

Check that your grip is not too strong. If your top hand is too far to the right (or left) you will see more than two to three knuckles on the back of your hand. More commonly it will be the bottom hand that causes the problem. Check that it is not too far underneath the club. Make sure that you're gripping with the fingers and not the palm of the bottom hand.

AIM AND ALIGNMENT

Check that your clubface is not aiming to the left (or right) of your intended target at address. With your alignment, it is vital to keep your feet, knees, hips and shoulders parallel to your target line. When you pull the ball it can be as simple a problem as being aligned too far to the left (or right). Remember your set up drill with the clubs on the ground to check alignment – try it now.

STANCE AND BALL POSITION

Check that you don't have too much weight on your front side during your set up. This can cause you to swing across

FAULTS

A strong grip may result in pulled shots.

Ensure the clubface isn't too closed.

Check alignment is not too far to the left.

the ball, which will lead to a pull. Additionally, the ball may be positioned too far forward in your stance, which would force you to lean forward to reach the ball and therefore open your shoulders too much to the left. This, again, will cause you to swing across your body, and can lead to a pull.

POSTURE

Ensure you do not have too much weight on your toes, or you will swing from out-to-in and pull the ball.

SWING

Presuming that you have checked all the set up points, and that you are still pulling your shots, you must have a swing fault. The main cause of a pull is swinging across the ball, which usually starts with a problem during the first move of your downswing. It often occurs when you are trying to hit the ball too hard, and is called "hitting from the top". The problem is caused when you try to gain power by hitting with your back shoulder. This causes the back elbow to separate from your body, which leads to an out-to-in swing.

To stop this happening you must feel that the first move of the downswing is your back elbow moving down toward your back hip. Practise this feeling, and refer back to the Pump and Swing Drill on pages 56–57.

Feel the rear elbow moving down to the rear hip.

Incorrect hitting from the top can create a pull.

Swinging outside the line can lead to a pull.

Ball too far forward.

THE HOOK

The hook is a very destructive shot because it starts quite straight or slightly right (or left if you're left-handed) of the target, and then bends viciously to the left (or right). If you hook the ball, it tends to fly very low and has a lot of roll when it hits the ground – the roll usually compounds the problem by taking the ball into trouble off the fairway. A hook is caused by swinging the club from inside-to-out of the ball-to-target line, with the clubface closed to that swing path at impact.

If you've developed a hooking shot, don't panic. Go through the GASPS changes here and you'll most likely find the cure.

GRIP
Check that your grip is not too strong – in other words, that your hands are not too far to the right (or left) on the club. If your top hand is too far round, you will see more than two to three knuckles on the back of your hand. More commonly it will be the bottom hand that causes the problem. Check that it is not too far underneath the club. Make sure you grip with the fingers and not the palm of the bottom hand.

AIM AND ALIGNMENT
Check that your clubface is not aiming to the left (or right) of your target at address. Keep your feet, knees, hips and shoulders parallel to your target line. People who hook tend to aim too far to the right (or left) to compensate for the ball's curve, which makes things worse – aim straight.

STANCE AND BALL POSITION
Ensure you don't have too much weight on your back foot at set up and don't have the ball too far back in your stance. Weight on the back foot, with the ball back in the stance, is a surefire recipe for a hook.

FAULTS

A hook is often caused by an overly strong grip.

Don't play the ball too far off the back foot.

Make sure your feet are correctly aligned.

POSTURE

Make sure that you are not standing too tall at address with too much weight on your heels. This will cause you to bring the club back too far on the inside, which can then make you attack the ball from the inside and hit a hook.

SWING

Presuming you are set up correctly, and you are still hooking, then your swing must be causing the problem. Swinging the club down into the ball from too far inside the target line is the most common swing fault that causes
a hook. To stop this, try the following exercise.
❶ Set up as normal, then pull your back foot backward about 8in (20cm) so that your feet are aiming way to the right (or left) of the target.
❷ Make sure your shoulders stay parallel to the ball-to-target line. This will feel a little strange, but don't worry. Hit some balls and try to feel that you are going to start the ball to the left (or right) of your target. This will make you feel that you are swinging across your body, and will really give you the correct feeling of turning through the ball.
❸ Practise this for a while, then go back to your normal set up position and hit some balls, trying to keep that same feeling of turning through the ball. This should help you to start swinging on a better line and get rid of the hook.

HOOK TIPS

- Check you don't have too much weight on your back foot.

- Ensure the ball is not set too far back in your stance.

- Don't stand too tall at address.

Really feel yourself swinging across your body (step 2).

FIXES

Set up with your back foot set behind the front (see step 1).

THE PUSH

The push is a shot that starts to the right of the target, and continues to head right throughout its flight (left for left-handed players). Although nowhere near as dramatic or potentially destructive as a hook, a push is very similar to the hook shot in that the club is traveling into the ball too far from the inside. The main difference between the two shots is that with the push the clubface is square or open to the swing path, as opposed to closed, as it would be for a hook.

Curing the push shot is quite simple – use the GASPS here.

GRIP
Check that your grip is not in a weak position. Remember that your top thumb should be just right (or left) of centre, and you should be able to see two to three knuckles on the back of your top hand. If your grip is too far round you will only see one knuckle or, in really bad cases, none at all. Your bottom hand grip should be in the fingers, with the palm of your hand facing the target. Do not let your bottom hand get too far on top of the club.

AIM AND ALIGNMENT
Check that your clubface is not aiming to the right (or left) of your intended target at address. With your alignment, it is vital to keep your feet, knees, hips and shoulders parallel to your target line. Being aligned too far to the right (or left) at address can be the main reason for the push creeping into your game.

STANCE AND BALL POSITION
Make sure that you do not have too much weight on your back foot at set up. Also, check that you do not have the

FAULTS

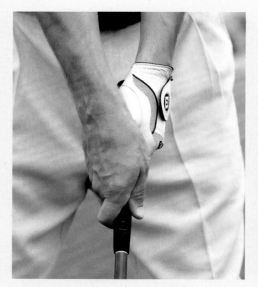

A weak grip may result in pushed shots.

Here the ball is too far back.

Check alignment of your feet.

ball too far back in your stance. If so, the clubface never has the chance to square up in the swing, leading to a push shot.

POSTURE

Check that you do not have too much weight on your heels when you set up. This will cause you to bring the club back too far on the inside, which can then make you attack the ball from the inside.

SWING

Presuming you are set up correctly, and you're still pushing your shots, then your swing must be causing the problem. Swinging the club down into the ball from too far inside the target line with an open clubface is the most common swing fault that causes a push. To feel that the clubface and body are moving through together – which will allow you to keep the clubface square – try the following exercise.

❶ Take your set up as normal, but now trap a towel under your armpits.
❷ Make a three-quarter length swing and try to knock some balls away. As you swing, try to feel that you are holding the towel in place. If your arms and body work independently, you will drop the towel.
❸ Practise this drill for a while, then remove the towel and hit some shots as normal. Your push should now have gone.

STRAIGHTENING TIPS

- Check your body is parallel to the target line.

- At set up, ensure your weight is evenly distributed.

- Ensure your arms and body work together as you swing.

FIXES

Place a towel around your chest, under your arms (see step 1).

Hold the towel in place as you swing (see step 2).

if your arms and body work together, the towel will stay in place (see step 3).

THE SHANK

Of all golf's bad shots, the shank is the most destructive shot in the game, and can lead people to despair. You even hear of people giving up golf because they can't get rid of the shank. A shank is when you hit the ball right out of the neck of an iron, where the shaft meets the head (the hosel). Because this part of the club is curved, it can make the ball fly off at all sorts of strange angles, usually about 45 degrees to the right or left.

SHANK TIPS

- Don't grip the club too tightly.

- Check you're not standing too close to the ball at address.

- Make sure the ball is in the correct position in your stance.

Standing too close to the ball.

Even a shank can be cured. As always, it takes patience and practice. Here are the GASPS you need to think about if you're suffering from a recurring shank.

GRIP

Check that you are not gripping the club too tightly. If you have hit a few shanks, it is very difficult to relax, but you must if you want to get rid of it.

AIM AND ALIGNMENT

Check that your clubface is not aiming to the right (or left for left-handers) of your intended target at address. A shank can be caused by either aligning your body too far to the left (or right), or too far to the right (or left) at address. Make sure that you set up parallel to your intended target line.

STANCE AND BALL POSITION

Make sure that you are not standing too close to the ball at address. If you stand too close, you are moving the clubhead closer to the ball, which can mean you hit your shots out of the neck. Make sure that the ball is in the correct position, just forward of centre.

POSTURE

Check that you have your weight on the balls of your feet. If you have your weight on your heels, you can fall forward to your toes during the swing, which will make you closer to the ball, and encourage the shank.

SWING

If you have checked all your set up positions, and you are still shanking, try the following exercise.

❶ Put a tee peg in the ground where the ball would be, and a tee on the same line but 2in (5cm) closer to you.

❷ Set up to the "ball" tee peg and, as you swing, try and hit the tee that is closer to you. This exaggerates the opposite swing to a shank, and gets the correct swing feeling.

❸ When you can consistently hit the inner tee, replace it with a ball and try to hit it in the same way.

❹ Finally, set up to the ball as normal, and try to hit some balls with the same swing feeling you have practised. Hopefully, your shank will be a thing of the past!

FIXES

Place two tee pegs in the ground about 2in (5cm) apart (see step 1).

Set up to the tee peg farthest from you (see step 2).

As you swing down, try to hit the tee peg nearest to you (see step 2).

HITTING THE GROUND

Although it is nowhere near as destructive or demoralising as a shank or hook, hitting the ground behind the ball (also known as hitting it fat or heavy), is still extremely frustrating – it results in a serious lack of distance, which in turn is likely to lead to a dropped shot. Do that once or twice a hole and you're losing anything between 18 and 32 strokes every time you play. If you are consistently hitting the ground behind the ball then there must be a fundamental error in either your set up or swing.

Check the GASPS techniques below for a quick way of losing this irritating habit.

GRIP
If you are not gripping the club tightly enough, then you could be losing control of the club during the course of your swing. This can be a cause of hitting the ball heavy.

AIM AND ALIGNMENT
Aim and alignment will be unlikely to cause you to hit the ground behind the ball.

STANCE AND BALL POSITION
Your stance might be too narrow, causing your body to sway during the swing. Check your ball position. If the ball is as little as an inch (2.5cm) too far forward and you make the perfect swing, you will hit the ground behind the ball.

POSTURE
One of the main reasons people hit the ground too early is that they dip their body on the downswing. However, you are forced to dip at the ball if your posture at set up is incorrect. If you stand too tall at address, you will be forced

FAULTS

Avoid standing too tall when addressing the ball.

Weight on the front foot when you swing back...

... will cause you to ground the club.

to dip into the ball, which can't be timed consistently. Make sure to adopt the correct posture, angle forward from the hips, and gently flex the knees.

SWING

If all the above set up points are correct, and you are still hitting the ground behind the ball, then the swing must be causing the problem. A common reason for hitting the ground behind the ball is a "reverse pivot". This happens when your weight moves in the wrong direction during your swing, so that at the top of your backswing your weight is on your front foot instead of your back foot. As you swing down, your weight is forced to shift back to your back foot, and this makes you dig the club into the ground behind the ball.

To stop this from happening you should try the following important drill.

❶ Put a tee in the ground where the ball would normally be and take your normal set up.
❷ As you reach the top of your backswing, lift your front foot off the ground by an inch or two (2.5–5cm). This will make sure that all your weight is on your back foot.
❸ As you start to swing down, replant your front foot, and, as you swing through and strike the ball, lift your

AVOIDING THE GROUND TIPS

• Grip the club tightly enough.

• Make sure your feet are shoulder width apart at set up.

• Make sure you weight moves back and through as you swing.

back foot off the ground. This might sound strange, and will feel very peculiar when you first try it, but it is a guaranteed way of getting the correct feeling of shifting your weight as you swing.
❹ Once you feel comfortable with this, replace the tee with a ball and try to hit a few shots. Finally, go back to your normal swing and you should automatically move your weight properly.

FIXES

Lift your front foot as you swing back (see step 2).

Then lift your rear foot (see step 3).

This will help you feel your weight transfer.

TOPPING

Hitting the ball above its centre, or equator, is known as topping or thinning the ball. Again, although not as dramatic as a shank or hook, topping will cause the ball to run along the ground, so losing a great deal of distance. This can ruin your scorecard if you repeat the problem too often. If you're consistently topping the ball, it's usually a sign of trying to help the ball into the air. This is a common error made by beginners and improving golfers who are anxious to see the ball flying high down the fairway.

Check the GASP set up points below, and if you have them all correct, try the swing drill at the bottom of the page.

GRIP

A possible cause of topping the ball is gripping the club too tight. This is quite a common mistake that people make, so if you are topping some shots, try and relax your grip.

AIM AND ALIGNMENT

Aim and alignment will be unlikely to cause you to hit the ground behind the ball.

STANCE AND BALL POSITION

Your stance might be too wide, causing a lack of leg action during the swing. Check that the ball is not too far back, or too far forward in your stance. Remember, with an iron, the ball should be just forward of centre.

POSTURE

Straightening the legs and body during the swing can cause you to swing higher than your set up position, and this will make you hit the top of the ball. The reason you would straighten your legs and body in your swing would be if you started too crouched over in your set up. Try to set up

FAULT

Don't crouch too low over the ball at set up.

FIX

Try to stand a little taller at address.

DISTANCE TIPS

- Don't stand with your feet too far apart at address.

- Don't crouch over the ball when you set up.

- Trust the loft of the club to lift the ball – don't try to lift it yourself.

a little taller than normal, and you should then be able to maintain a constant height throughout the swing.

SWING

Presuming that you have checked all the above set up points, and that you are still topping the ball, the most likely swing problem is that you are trying to lift the ball at impact and help it into the air. You must trust the club to lift the ball
for you. To make good contact with an iron, you actually need to hit down slightly on the ball. You should never swing up in an attempt to lift the ball, as you will hit it half way up and top it.

To get out of this fault, you need to develop a feeling of squeezing the ball into the ground. Try this drill.

❶ Go to the practice ground and try to hit some shots with a 6- or 7-iron.
❷ As you hit the shots, try to feel that you are going to take a step forward toward the target just after impact.

This "walk-through" drill really makes you swing down and through instead of up. Legendary golfer Gary Player actually used to play several shots with this technique.

FIXES

Practise taking a step toward the target ...

... just after striking the ball (see step 2).

RULES AND ETIQUETTE

RULES OF THE GAME

There are more rules for golf than for any other game. In fact, there is a whole book of them produced every few years by the Royal and Ancient Golf Club of St. Andrews in Scotland and the United States Golf Association. No one knows all the rules, but you should try and get a copy of the rules from your local club and carry them in your golf bag to refer to when necessary. Listed over the next few pages are the most common ones that you should learn in order to play the game properly.

GENERAL RULES
• Put an identification mark on your ball. If you cannot identify it in the rough you have to presume it is lost, so make sure you know which ball is yours.
• You must only have a maximum of 14 clubs in your bag.
• You are not allowed to ask for advice from anyone other than your caddie or partner.
• Do not practise on the course during a round. (This does not include practice swings taken before playing your shot.)
• Check if there is a dress code for your club – they may prohibit the wearing of shorts, for example.

PLAYING THE BALL
• Play the ball as you find it. Do not move it unless a rule permits it.
• Do not improve your lie or stance by bending or breaking any branches, or stamping the ground down near your ball.
• Do not touch the ground or sand with your clubhead in a hazard or bunker until you make contact with the ball.
• Make sure you play the correct ball. If you play the wrong ball by mistake it is a two-shot penalty.
• Unplayable Ball – you can declare this at any time. It will be a one-shot penalty and you are entitled to drop the ball in one of three possible locations; the choice is yours:
❶ You can drop within two clubs' length of where your ball was lying when you declared it unplayable. This must be no nearer the hole.
❷ You can go back as far as you want, keeping the point where the ball was between you and the hole.
❸ You can go back to the place from where you played your previous shot.

Moving an unplayable ball.

LOST BALL OR BALL OUT OF BOUNDS
A very common rule, especially when you are learning!

If you lose your ball, or hit it out of bounds (which is normally marked by white posts) you must take a penalty of stroke and distance. This means you have a one-shot penalty, and must go back to where you played your last shot, to play your next shot. For example, if you hit your tee shot out of bounds, you must play another ball from the tee, and it is now your third shot.

There are set instructions for taking a drop.

PROVISIONAL BALL

If you hit a shot that you think may be lost or may be out of bounds, you are entitled to play a provisional ball to save you walking all the way back if you can't find your ball. For example, if you hit your tee shot into long rough, you are entitled to hit a provisional ball. If you find the first ball, then you pick up the provisional. If you can't find the first ball, you then play the provisional (remember you will now be playing your fourth shot because of the lost-ball penalty).

If you do hit a provisional ball, you must inform the other players that it is a provisional ball. Failure to inform them means that as soon as you hit the "provisional" ball, it immediately becomes the ball in play, even if you find the first one. An expensive error!

MOVABLE OBSTRUCTIONS

If a movable obstruction interferes with your stance or swing, you can move it out of the way. If your ball moves, you can replace it with no penalty.

A movable obstruction is as it sounds – an artificial obstruction that can be moved. For example it can be a rake, a tee marker, a bench not bolted down, and so on.

IMMOVABLE OBSTRUCTION

If an immovable obstruction interferes with your stance or swing, you are entitled to a "free drop" (see Taking a Drop, below) within one club's length of the nearest point of relief (the closest point to where the ball lies that gives you complete relief from the obstruction).

An immovable obstruction is an artificial article that can't be moved, i.e. a cart path or a bolted-down bench.

TAKING A DROP

Whenever you take a drop, either under penalty (unplayable ball) or without penalty (to drop away from an immovable obstruction) you should follow these instructions.

❶ Mark the original position of the ball.
❷ Stand erect, and hold your arm out at shoulder height and drop the ball.

A dropped ball must be redropped if it rolls into a hazard, onto the green, out of bounds, or nearer the hole. If you drop the ball twice and it rolls closer to the hole twice, you should place the ball as close as possible to where it made ground contact on the second drop.

GOLFING ETIQUETTE

Despite the fact that golf has become a modern game enjoyed by all people, it still holds many traditional values and standards. These values help to make golf the game it is, and if you are new to the game it is important that you learn them and adhere to them every time you play. Most exist for very good commonsense reasons and help to make sure the game is played fairly. General consideration for others is extremely important, and if you follow the guidelines set out below you will have no problems.

GENERAL ETIQUETTE
• Do not move, talk, or make unnecessary noise when other players are hitting their shots.
• Do not stand too close to or directly behind the ball when a player is about to play.
• Do not take mobile phones or other electrical devices onto the course.
• If marking a card, record the score after each hole, but do so on the next tee so as not to hold up players behind waiting to play.

PACE OF PLAY
Pace of play is a real problem in the modern game. Rounds seem to take longer and longer. Please be aware of this, as nothing is more frustrating than having to wait to play on every shot.
• You should always aim to keep up with the game in front.
• If you are lagging behind, and the people behind are waiting for you, then stand aside and let them play through.
• Avoid having too many practice swings. One is enough.
• When you get to the green, leave your bags on the side closest to the next tee.
• When all your group have putted out, leave the green immediately.
• If you think your ball may be lost, make sure that you play a provisional.
• If you have lost a ball and are searching for it, then let the players behind play through.

CARE OF THE COURSE
It is every player's responsibility to ensure all care is afforded to the course at all times.

ON THE TEE
• Avoid taking divots from practice swings on the tee. If possible, have your practice swing away from the tee.
• Do not replace divots on tees – they are sanded and seeded by green keepers on a regular basis.
• Do not take your trolley onto the tee – leave it at the side.

Remain still when other people are putting.

Go through your pre-shot routine when setting up a shot.

FAIRWAY AND ROUGH
• Always replace any divots that you make with either a practice or normal swing.

BUNKERS
• Always enter and exit the bunker from the lowest side.
• Use the rakes provided to rake over all the areas that you have roughed up.
• Place the rake outside the bunker at the place least likely for it to affect any shots from other players.

ON THE GREEN
• Do not take bags or trolleys on the green.
• If your ball has made a mark when it hit the green, use a pitch mark repairer to correct the damage.
• Do not drag your feet and scuff the green. Avoid walking on the line of another player's putt.

• Do not lean on your putter because it will leave an indentation on the green.
• Replace the flag carefully when all players have putted out.

If you follow these guidelines every time you play, not only will you enjoy your game more, so will everyone else playing on the course that day.

GLOSSARY

Ace Hole completed in a single stroke.

Address The position assumed over the golf ball before striking it.

Albatross A score of three under par on a single hole.

Alignment The way that the body is positioned prior to a strike in relation to an imagined ball-to-target line.

Approach Shot played to the green from the fairway or rough.

Back nine Second set of nine holes on an 18-hole course; "INS" on scorecard.

Backspin Anti-clockwise spin on ball.

Backswing Initial part of the swing.

Birdie A score of one under par on a single hole.

Bite How well a backspin shot stops when the ball lands on the green.

Blind shot When the final target cannot be viewed.

Bogey A score of one over par on a single hole.

Bunker A depression that tends to be filled with sand; used as a hazard.

Caddie A non-playing person who advises a golfer and carries the bags.

Carry Distance between where the ball is hit to where it first strikes the course.

Clubface Grooved part of clubhead that is used to strike the ball.

Clubhead Lower part of golf club that is used to strike the ball.

Cross-handed Putting grip where left hand is below the right hand.

Cut shot Slicing the ball to produce a curving left-to-right shot.

Deliberate draw Low shot where the ball starts marginally to the right of the target then curves back to the centre.

Deliberate fade A shot where the ball starts marginally to the left of the target then curves back to the centre.

Divot Piece of turf cut by clubhead.

Dogleg A hole in which the fairway dramatically bends.

Double bogey A score of two over par on a single hole.

Double eagle A score of three under par on a single hole.

Downswing Shift from backswing through to the initial impact.

Drive Shot played from the tee.

Driver Club used to hit the ball the furthest, usually from the tee.

Driving range Practice area to try and improve hitting the ball from a tee.

Eagle A score of two strokes under par on a single hole.

Fairway Finely mown grass area between the tee and the green.

Flagstick Sits in the hole to mark target.

Flat swing Backswing where the club is more horizontal and vertical.

Flight The way the ball moves in the air.

Follow through Final part of the swing, after the ball has been hit.

Front nine First set of nine holes on an 18-hole course; "OUTS" on scorecard.

Full set The 14 clubs allowed to be used while playing golf.

Green Site of the flagstick and hole.

Grip Upper part of the club that is held in the hands of a golfer.

Half set The seven clubs used by beginners when playing golf.

Handicap A number issued to a player that reflects their individual ability level and is used to make matches start evenly.

Hazards Lateral or water obstructions marked by stakes or lines.

Hole 1. Area between the tee and the green. 2. To putt the ball. 3. The cup that holds the flagstick.

Hole in one When a hole is completed in a single stroke.

Hook A shot where the ball starts marginally to the right of the target then dramatically curves to the left.

Hosel Socket that connects clubhead to the shaft of a golf club.

Hybrid club Golf club that is a cross between an iron and a wood; also called rescue clubs and utility clubs.

Impact When the clubface meets the ball during a full swing.

Interlocking grip Style of grip when the right hand's little finger intertwines with the left hand's forefinger.

Iron Type of club used for majority of shots between tee and green.

Lie 1. Angle between clubhead and shaft. 2. How the ball rests in relation to grass, ground or sand around it.

Line Direction that player aims to strike the ball.

Lob shot High and short hit of the ball played with backspin to avoid hazards.

Loft 1. Measurement of the angle of the clubhead. 2. The height that a player puts on a shot.

Lost ball If a ball is hit out of bounds or cannot be found, a one-shot penalty occurs and the player replays shot.

Net Score after handicaps deducted.

Par Standard score for an individual hole.

Pin Sits in the hole to mark the target.

Pitch High and short approach shot that lands softly.

Pitching wedge Short iron with a high degree of loft; useful for chipping.

Provisional ball An additional golf ball used when a lost ball is highly likely.

Push A shot where the ball travels straight to the right, without curving.

Push slice A shot where the ball starts marginally to the right of the target then curves to the right.

Putter Type of club used for hitting the ball in the closing stages of the hole.

Reading the green Examination of the slope and contours of the putting area.

Rough Area outside the fairway that is used to deter and penalise players.

Run How far a ball travels after initially hitting the ground.

Sand wedge A club used for chipping, pitching and escaping from bunkers.

Shaft Long extension of the club from grip to clubhead.

Shank A shot that is hit in error off the neck or hosel of the club.

Slice A shot where the ball starts marginally to the left of the target then dramatically curves to the right.

Square 1. An equal score between players or teams. 2. To position the clubface and/or feet at right angles to the imaginary ball-to-target line.

Sweet spot Most effective hitting area.

Takeaway The start of the backswing.

Thin shot A strike where the ball travels low but without accuracy.

Vardon grip Most common style of grip, when the right hand's little finger overlaps the left hand's forefinger.

Wood A club used for long shots, from the tee and fairway.

INDEX